A Wayward Traveler book:

AMERICAN LITERARY NOMADS

ISBN: 979-8989343041

Available on Amazon, ACX,
Ingram, KDP, and other retailers.

Published in print, hardcover, eBook & audiobook.

Cover Design by Andrew Holman
www.andrewholman.com

Interior Illustrations by Tom Fish
tfishart@yahoo.com

Compass Logo design by Ky and Moon McMillan
thekylemc@gmail.com

American Literary Nomads

My Road Less Traveled...

This story is semi-autographical. You can call it fiction if it makes
you feel better, but it all happened. It was crafted as a blend of
several road trips, with real and imagined characters
riding along on a journey east.

Initially, I penned an Author's Note to explain my state of mind,
but then I faltered and moved it to the end of the book.
It's there now if you feel the need…

Skeleton Mesa and beyond is Navajo Mountain, AZ.

Table of Contents

Book List   page 11

Chapter One – Sedona   page 17

Chapter Two – Arizona   page 35

Chapter Three – Utah   page 57

Chapter Four – Colorado   page 75

Chapter Five – North Dakota   page 99

Chapter Six – Iowa   page 117

Chapter Seven – Kansas   page 135

Chapter Eight – Ohio   page 153

Chapter Nine – Massachusetts   page 171

Chapter Ten – Maine   page 191

Author's Note   page 207

Dedication – Benny & Pat   page 209

Illustrations – Tom Fish   page 213

Acknowledgements   page 215

Biography & Other Books by RLD   page 219

American Literary Nomads

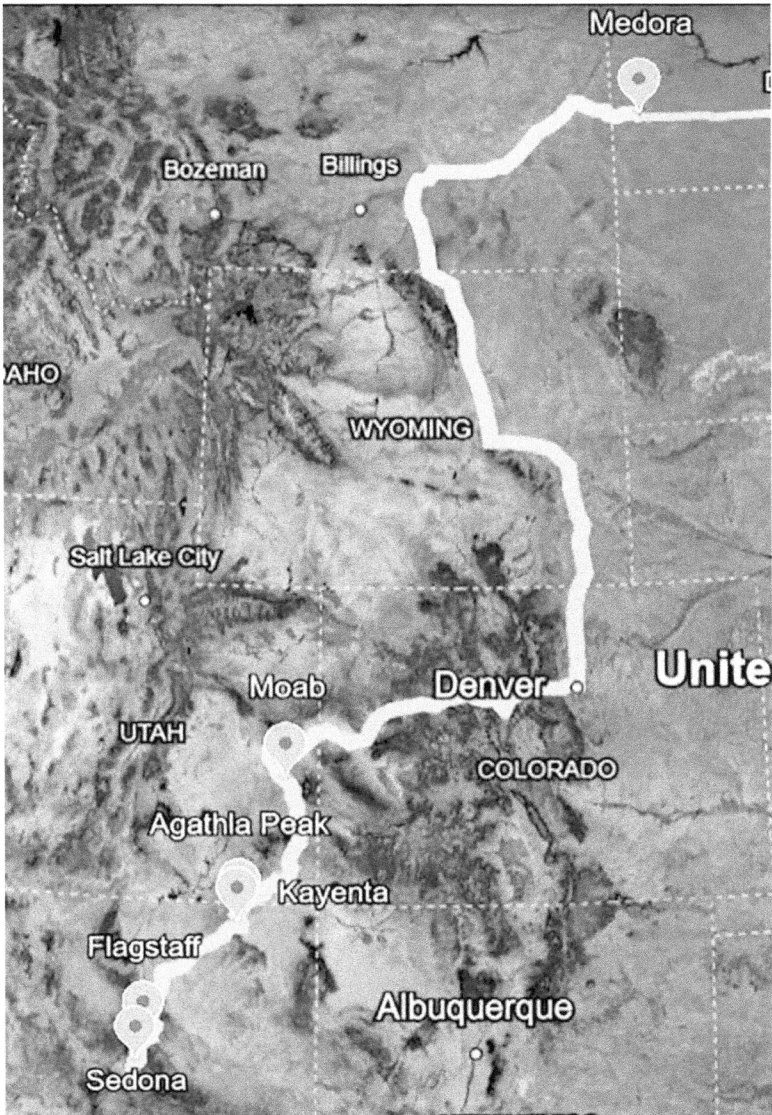

Map 1: Sedona, Arizona to Medora, North Dakota.
(1,413 miles.)

Forest Gump Point, Utah.

I'm so happy 'cause today I found my friends, they're in my head.
(Kurt Cobain, Lithium)

Book List for American Nomads:

John Steinbeck – *Travels with Charlie*

Everett Ruess – *A Vagabond for Beauty*

Edward Abbey – *The Fool's Progress*

Robert Pirsig – *Zen and the Art of Motorcycle Maintenance*

Theodore Roosevelt – *Ranch Life and the Hunting Trail*

Walt Whitman – *Leaves of Grass*

Mark Twain – *A Boy's Ambition* or *Roughing It*

Ernest Hemmingway – *Big two-hearted River*

Henry David Thoreau – *Walden* or *The Maine Woods*

Joseph Campbell – *The Hero with a Thousand Faces*

Additional Reading

Summerset Maugham – *The Razor's Edge*

Jon Krakauer – *Into The Wild*

Bruce Chatwin – *Anatomy of Restlessness*

Paul Theroux – *Figures in a Landscape: People and Places*

Cheryl Strayed – *Wild*

Neil Peart – *Ghost Rider*

Bud Holmstrom – *The Doing of the Thing*

Bill Bryson – *The Lost Continent*

William Least Heat-Moon – *Blue Highways*

Books to Avoid

Jack Kerouac – *On the Road*

Shel Silverstein – *The Giving Tree*

John Steinbeck and Charlie.
(1902 – 1968)

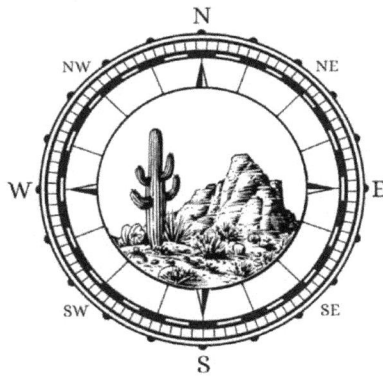

Thunder Mountain in snow, Sedona, Arizona.

Chapter One

SEDONA

On the morning of my intended departure, I stop by the stupa. I'm full of dread and hope I might find some peace here. I follow a trail that skirts outside the main area, trying to stay away from any tourists — and then I notice a path I've never taken before.

It leads to a medicine wheel. I can't believe I've never spotted it in twenty years.

I stare at it a moment, trying to remember what I can about the wheels. I know there are hundreds of these wheels spread across America, and some are thousands of years old. The circular shape has spokes radiating outward, dividing it into four quadrants, representing the four seasons, the cardinal directions, and even the stages of life.

There is a plaque with instructions on intentions and how to use the medicine wheel, but I'm too caught up in myself to stop and read. Instead, I start slowly walking around the wheel, trying to figure it out as I go.

I step slowly, the beaten path disappearing into the heat. It's only 10:00 am, but the Arizona sun is blaring down through a cloudless, cerulean sky. Of course, I don't have a hat, glasses or sunscreen. Having lived in the southwest, I almost never hike away from the coolness of sunrise or sunset — but here I am. There's some reason why my body wants to punish itself, but I can't figure it out.

I can tell I'm not doing it right, too. I keep walking, lost in my own thoughts. I feel like I'm charging with negative energy, not relaxing. My brain is spinning so much that I suddenly realize I've been doing this for twenty minutes — I feel dehydrated.

Then, as I complete another circle, I go to take one more step, trip over myself, and fall right out of the medicine wheel. I stand up and brush myself off. I'm no mystic, but that sure felt like a sign.

I begin to drive home, and before I'm halfway there, I'm angry.

I shout out the window, "Twenty-plus years here, Sedona, and that's how you're gonna send me off? You kicking me out?"

When I get home, I stare at my pile of gear and feel unprepared for the journey I'm about to embark on. My lower back aches, my legs are shaky, and there's a lump in my throat.

I look around and shout, "I'm leaving."

Nothing. Our heavy conversations from the night before still linger in the air like tattered spiderwebs. Will she really get her own place? I add, "Might be gone a few weeks…"

More silence. We both agreed this road trip would be good for me; maybe I'll sort out a few things, but what's on the other side?

Then, she appears in the hallway. She looks into my eyes and sees I'm agitated. She smiles sadly. I'm about to leave when she says, "You should take the dog?"

My mind churns with what complications that might entail, but at the same time, I'm relieved to have a companion. She disappears down the hallway, and I begin loading the car.

Within a few trips, I've gotten most of it. After one run, the door slams behind me, louder than I would have liked. My wife says something, but the dog begins barking madly, obscuring her comments. Over the coming days, I wonder what she said.

As I stagger out to the car, both hands full of gear with a small pack slipping off my left shoulder, I'm sure I look drunk. But that isn't it — I wish I were drunk — I'm just enraged, and I don't really know where the anger is coming from. "Chill out, Roman!" I yell.

After tossing the pack and other bundles into the backseat, I return to the house. Unfortunately, by this time, the dog has run to the other end of the building to see me through the side window.

You'd think it was the end of the world the way he's going on.

I whistle and then shout, "Come on, Dummy!"

Soon, a small, shaggy critter comes skidding around the corner. He is a poodle, shiatsu, and pomeranian mix with an underbite. Small and hyper, he only weighs about fifteen pounds — when wet, he looks like a drowned squirrel.

I walk him to the car. Open the door.

He gets in and gives me a look that clearly says, "Thanks for not leaving me, Bro."

There's a plastic milk crate on the passenger seat half-filled with books: my reading list over the last year. I'm tempted to toss it in the driveway — those books are a big part of my downfall — but instead, I set it on the floor so Roman can have a seat up front.

He ignores the offered spot and jumps on the console between the seats.

I hop in the car, gun the gas, and leave before my wife changes her mind about the dog.

We cross West Sedona and its seven lights, then wend our way through the two roundabouts. Soon, we pass through Uptown and the hordes of tourists. They gawk at the vermillion cliffs that frame the town and stagger back into the road while taking photos.

It's tempting to nick one of them with my car, but I refrain.

Momentarily, we're on 89a, making our way up Oak Creek Canyon, and I breathe a sigh of relief. There are still tourists here — and their vehicles — but they're spread out now, and the backdrop of the canyon walls behind them is breathtaking. For a brief moment, I remember what drew me here over twenty years ago.

Roman is now settled in and curled up in the passenger seat. Sometimes, I doubt he even realizes he's in a moving vehicle. I look over at him, and I'm so glad he's here — without him, I'd be completely alone. By myself. Yikes.

Having a companion keeps my mind from wandering. Grounds me in the present—at least for a little while. That's good for a guy like me because, left alone long enough, you never know where my mind will drift.

These days, I'm a churning mass of regret, health problems, financial stress and marital issues. No wonder my wife seemed so supportive of my road trip. She's happy to get rid of me, and I have a sinking feeling that she might prefer I didn't come back.

And two-thirds of my daughters are currently mad at me, so I can't expect sympathy from them. How did I get here?

I stare at Roman and ask, "Did we forget anything?"

He shrugs, and I imagine him saying, "Might have been better if you'd left all that emotional baggage back in Sedona."

For a little dog, he can be cutting in his remarks. I'd match different words to his strange glances and looks, but I'm being honest here and simply telling you what pops up in my head.

He gives me a last confused gaze and asks, "Why? Are we going somewhere?"

We are leaving Sedona and the high desert for the great plateau—the Colorado! It covers one hundred thirty thousand square miles, big sections of four states, and most of it sits six thousand feet above sea level. To get there, I will traverse thirty miles of canyons rising three thousand feet in elevation. I usually love this drive, but I'm tense as a piano string today. I try to forget the medicine wheel.

I attempt to let the canyon work its magic and concentrate on steadily breathing. Why do we supposedly take twenty thousand breaths a day, but sometimes, a half-dozen can take an eternity? I'm nervous and do all my tricks: focus on the guardrails, count my inhalations, and hold the wheel at ten and two.

Alongside the road, the creek trickles. The air is moist and cool, saturated with the sweet smell of pine and juniper. Ghostly sycamores cast us in a mix of shade and dappled sunshine. There's something eternal here. We cruise along.

I flip on the radio and catch Harry Nilsson singing…

Everybody's talking at me, I don't hear a word they're saying
Only the echoes of my mind.

There's something haunting about these lyrics…

People stopping, staring, I can't see their faces,
Only the shadows of their eyes.

I crack a window as the chorus plays. The scent pulls my little dog around. He climbs on the console again and tries to look casual.

I'm going where the sun keeps shining, Through the pouring rain
Going where the weather suits my clothes

Banking off of the northeast winds, Sailing on a summer breeze
And skipping over the ocean like a stone

Eventually, the agave and desert oak give way to higher-altitude plants, and the pinion pines cower and fade before the stately old ponderosas. A ribbon of cobalt blue flows high above me. Sandstone layers call out from the depths: burgundy and maroon where the creek cuts deep, rising to cinnabar and crimson. Finally, high above, yellowish-white, nearly luminescent rocks ascend to the plateau's rim, which is capped by a black layer of volcanic basalt.

A gust of chilled wind reminds me it's September. I sense the seasons changing and wonder what's still alive in the canyon. Plenty rustling about in the desert fall air, but not many critters. Yellowed sycamore leaves. Crumpled brown ferns. A flash of red from a maple along the water. Summer has ended, and Fall will pass in the blink of an eye. You can feel it at this altitude—currently about five thousand feet and climbing.

I glimpse a grey heron on the creek's banks and then a large raven pecking at the remains of a ringtail that got hit in the night. There may still be a lot of life out there, but there's also plenty of death and decay. It's scary how lifeless a location can feel once winter sets in; how a physical place can suddenly become an echo of itself.

And I'm not just talking about plants and animals. How many people lived and died in this canyon? Going back over the eons… hundreds? Thousands? When the seasons change, I sense their presence, their spirits, and their voices echoing off the rocks.

See where my mind wanders when left on its own? It's not all that healthy. I should return to observing nature, but the underlying history always gets me. I should say white history in this case. There are a half-dozen substantial Sinaguan ruins in the Verde Valley, but none in the canyon. And the Apache didn't leave much of a trace after them. We don't know much about who lived here in pre-history. If you weren't one of a half-dozen white guys who arrived in the last hundred and fifty years, then you get forgotten altogether. Not even a footnote.

Oak Creek Canyon swallows its past like parched earth takes in water. There is a wave of death each fall, and then the spring rains and flooding creek wash it clean.

Still, on a few particular bends of this winding road, I sometimes see flickers of a few of the former residents I do know about. I'll admit that I have an active imagination, and occasionally, there's a little marijuana involved, but I'm telling you, I actually see these apparitions. Mostly, it's Bear Howard, one of the first men to settle here, or J.J. Thompson, another pioneer. Both were men haunted by their past and then found a home in the beautiful canyon.

On gloomy days, I sometimes glimpse Richard Wilson, an Arkansas bear hunter who got himself killed by pursuing—and then cornering—one of the last grizzlies in this area with only a small gun. He wears an unsettling expression as I cruise past.

And he should, I reckon, going after a big bear like that with a squirrel gun.

I guess I'm just sore that the bears are gone in the first place: the Mexican Grizzly has been extinct in the Southwest since the 1930s.

Ever see one of those old Remington drawings of cowboys on horseback fighting a dusty, silver grizzly bear? That was most likely a Mexican Grizzly. There may be a few stuffed specimens in a museum in Mexico City. Other than that, we can only hope they clone them someday. At this point, half my dreams lay in cloning — or self-drive cars. How I'd like to tilt my seat back, take a nap, and wake up at my destination.

If only my destination were a bit clearer.

It's a beautiful fall day, but I'm not taking any pictures.

Instead, I glance at my cell. I'm tempted to call my wife or one of the daughters, but it's really come to a time when I have to face these fears by myself.

I turn it off and toss it in the glovebox — off for the foreseeable future.

I'm just driving up the canyon, heading north. I'm not sure where I'll go after that. It doesn't matter, I suppose. As Steinbeck suggested in *Travels with Charley*, always begin a long journey by starting in the opposite direction of your final objective.

Although I feel a more appropriate Steinbeck quote for my current situation — that of drifting almost randomly across the West — is:

People don't take trips, trips take people.

John Steinbeck knew he was dying in 1962 and wanted to see the country one last time before he did. *Travels with Charley* is his account of that journey, completed in a modified truck and camper he named Rocinante (after Don Quixote's horse). Charley, his companion, was a standard poodle. He completed his road trip when he was sixty and died six years later.

When I think of Steinbeck's perspective in that book, it depresses me. He seemed happy and content, like he'd waited all his life to take that casual drive. To finally find his path.

I'm the opposite. I feel like I'm limping out of town — running from something rather than looking for it. But everything I was doing seemed only to cloud the situation. Make the hole deeper.

I have tried to find my way by examining the lives of others. I've written three historical fiction books: one about a sickly rich kid who wanted to take on the world, another about a dreamer who wanted to embrace it, and a final one about a guy who tried to escape it. I consider those men to be my brothers now — I understand them profoundly — but I can't follow their leads. Like it or not, modern nomads must find their own way.

I remember a former editor trying to explain the difference between the words "path" and "trail" and saying, "It's better to be on the trail of an elephant than in its path." I'd like to imagine I'm blazing my own path, but the truth is, I feel more like I'm the elephant, just charging forward.

Maybe I'm simply getting old. But the more I see of old age, the more I want no part of it. It seems like a tale of diminishing returns. Yet you can't wish for a timely death when you have children — especially when some of them are barely adults. And what will I leave them anyway? Certainly, not enough cash for them to relax. A curio cabinet full of memories and recollections of a thousand stories. Sometimes, it seems enough, but other days, it feels empty.

And, like many of the men and women I know, I think I've somehow failed at life despite the many attempts to *Follow my Bliss*, as Joseph Campbell used to say.

We're high up in the canyon now, nearing the switchbacks, but I'm still anxious. I question whether I can make this drive. I guess I don't trust myself when I launch into a new adventure — but who can blame me? A half-dozen times, I've gone off into the mountains intending to hike a hundred miles or so. In every one of those instances, I limped off the trail in horrible shape. In the worst of them, I lost a quarter of my body weight. Dysentery, giardia, malaria, dengue fever, leeches… the list goes on.

I'm no spring chicken, either. I've got a list of ailments: gout, GERD, arthritis, a failed bunionectomy on my left foot, and a forty-year-old lumbar fusion that aches when I push myself too far. However, my biggest problem has always been my mind. Restless and unforgiving, it dwells on the past while fearing the future. I question everything. Unfortunately, past successes seem to have no bearing on my confidence level when considering my future.

If I had a little religion, I might have a place to turn, but I'm also alone there. I'm an apostate. I think God is an experience, not a conscious entity or some grand puppet master. As a young man, I became obsessed with the idea that God could—and should—fix some of the injustices on this planet. It's one of the reasons I began traveling. But the more I saw the horrors of humanity, the more I blamed it on God. I grew tired of empty promises about salvation and eternal life. I decided then that if I could overthrow God, I would.

That alone put stress between me and my relatives, most of them dedicated Catholics who seemed almost to yearn for the day they will be admitted into Heaven. Nobody likes a downer, especially if he's raining on a plan you've made for years.

Honestly, I don't think about God much these days—only when I'm in a dark mood and need venting. Then he suddenly becomes the realist thing around me.

I feel like Henry Lightcap, Edward Abbey's protagonist in *The Fool's Progress*. In that semi-autobiographical novel, Lightcap makes his way across the country with a dying dog, trying to reach his ancestral home in West Virginia while ranting about "progress" the whole way there.

Roman gives me a desperate look and says, "Easy on the dying dog stuff—I'm only seven."

We're on the plateau now, cruising along at about seven thousand feet. We drive ten miles through a towering ponderosa pine forest with yellow aspen mixed in. I see a sign for the interstate and also 7-11 up ahead. An erratic wind tosses my car about. My arms tense up. My heart begins to race, and my breathing quickens.

I approach the 7-11, just before the highway, and I can't look away as we pass it. It's like my head is in a vice.

In the parking lot, a middle-aged guy in a business suit leans against a dark blue Buick Skylark. He's eating a breakfast burrito and smiling like it's the best day of his life. He grins, nods as I pass, and then waves with a ketchup-covered finger.

With effort, my head snaps forward. I try to ignore what I just saw. Pretend he's a figment of my imagination. He's one of the reasons I'm leaving.

I shout, "Fuck you, Bill!"

I turn onto I-40, heading east. I'll only be on it for a few exits as I want to spend as little time on big highways on this drive as possible. I've crossed North America twenty-two times — been back and forth across I-40 like a yoyo. Wherever I go in this country, the ghosts of my past follow me. I often imagine my youngest daughter sitting beside me... an eleven-year-old who never ages. She's there now, looking just as she did a few years back when we made the long drive to the cabin in Maine together.

I glance over at her and say, "Shrek and Donkey..."

And she replies, "... on the road again."

Slowly, she fades, and I find myself staring at Roman.

"You hungry?" I ask, knowing he's always hungry.

We exit and turn onto Route 66. This highway was a primary route for crossing America for much of the twentieth century. It stretched from Chicago to Los Angeles; established in the twenties, no cross-country trip was complete without spending some time on it. On forgotten stretches, I sometimes glimpse the shadows of the masses of farm workers who used it during the Dust Bowl.

We pull into the Dog Haus, and Roman glances at me.

"Is this your pathetic attempt at living dangerously?" his eyes ask. But then he softens, and I know he's remembering the time we came here when I shared a hotdog with him.

"Don't worry," I say, "we're both gonna break the rules today."

I order two dogs: a little Tabasco, no ketchup, and hold the mayo.

While I wait, I read an article framed and mounted to the wall.

There used to be a pay phone on the location, and Jackson Browne used it back in the seventies while waiting for his car to be repaired in Winslow. One day, a woman in a Toyota pickup cruised past him, and the image stuck.

A few years later, when Glenn Frey was helping him write a song called *Take it Easy*, he recollected the event, and the rest is history. The lyrics play in my head while I wait for our dogs...

> *Well, I'm a-runnin' down the road*
> *try'n to loosen my load*
> *I've got seven women on my mind...*

I chuckle because I have at least seven women on my mind. But it's hard not to—I'm halfway there with a wife, three daughters, and a mother, sister and granddaughter. Plus, our business employs nine women. In Sedona, I swim in a sea of estrogen.

But I'm not going to share all that stuff with you. This is my trip—my headtrip—and even though I might talk about them occasionally, I'd like to keep the girls out of it. So, when I talk about my daughters, it'll be Number 1, Number 2 or Number 3. You don't need to know their names. They're between thirteen and twenty-five, Number 1 is the oldest, and so on...

And when I talk about my wife... well, I will try my best not to talk about my wife for now.

I grab our hotdogs and get back on Route 66. I break one in two and give half to Roman. He wolves it down in two bites, like other dogs are just waiting to steal from him. The Tabasco has him licking his chops. "Easy there, buddy," I say. "Pace yourself."

He grins back. "You should talk."

When I put the car in gear, he jumps up on the console between seats and gives me his best smile.

I shake my head, "It's your funeral." We've gone over this before, Roman and I. He loves standing on the console, but the problem is, when I hit the brakes, he goes flying forward into the AC/Stereo unit. Each time, he acts surprised—like he has no memory of the last time. My wife would have him buckled and riding in a little padded crate, but as I said, we're living dangerously, so I allow him to take chances.

A few miles up the road, I turn onto Route 89, heading north toward Lake Powell and the Grand Canyon. I gobble down the rest of the second hot dog while Roman eyeballs me. It doesn't take long for me to wish I'd opted for a healthier lunch, but that's the price you pay for being rebellious at my age.

I've got about sixty miles to go before my turnoff at Tuba City. I hoped I'd be settling into the road trip now, but I'm not. A storm rages in my head, and I can't turn it off. I know I control these voices, so why won't they be quiet? I can't relax. Roman can sense it and gives me a worried look.

After ten miles, I turn off at the Sunset Crater scenic loop.
I channel more of the *Take it Easy* lyrics.

Take it easy, take it easy
Don't let the sound of your own wheels drive you crazy
Lighten up while you still can
Don't even try to understand
Just find a place to make your stand, and take it easy...

But it's no good. I feel like I'm still staggering around that medicine wheel in the heat. Everything is spinning.

I slam on the brakes on a bend in the road near an ash-covered volcanic hill. Roman is airborne and scrambling to get his feet under him while we skid off the road. I unbuckle and jump out of the car.

Roman tries to follow and gets a door slammed in his face.

He watches sadly as I stagger up the crater, sinking to my knees and then vanishing.

28

Five minutes later, I'm alone in the barren wilderness. I've stumbled into a small hollow. There's nothing but ash and dead trees around me. I angrily look up at the sky and begin tearing off my clothes.

Soon, I'm naked and red-faced. My anger seems to know no bounds.

I look up at the heavens and scream at the top of my lungs, over and over, until I'm hoarse, and then sink to my knees sobbing.

Sunset Crater, Arizona.

Everett Ruess and Curly riding a burro.
(1914 – 1934?)

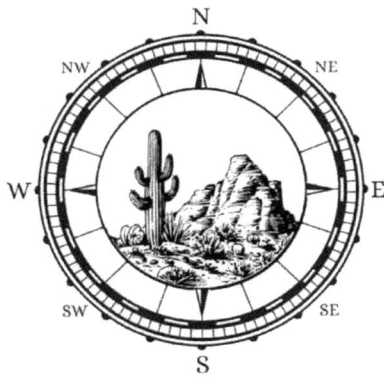

The Painted Desert, Arizona.

Chapter Two

ARIZONA

*B*ack in the car later, I feel guilty, like a Steppenwolf the next morning, hungover and unsure of what happened. I have these episodes occasionally — usually in remote places for some reason — and they always confuse me.

Sometimes, I think it's my mind lashing out because of the violence I experienced when I was younger. For instance, I was once beaten unconscious when trying to flee a mob. I was delirious with fever, suffering from hepatitis — as was most of the mob — and kept running into street signs because my vision was blurred.

That's a psychological scar with no physical remnants other than nightmares, but when I'm on a busy city sidewalk and I have to navigate around a street sign, I get flashes of that day.

But it doesn't explain the outbursts. Or the anger.

And there's Bill, of course. I suppose he's still out there, but we'll try to forget about him for a while.

Most times, I try to cover my tracks by losing myself in a buzz, and I do that with a vape pen as I turn right onto 89, heading towards the Grand Canyon and Lake Powell again.

On my left is a ponderosa forest with the snow-capped San Francisco peaks towering behind them. At 12,633 feet, they're the highest mountains around, rising above Flagstaff, which sits at 7,000 feet. Sometimes, they keep their snow year-round. I can see them from Sedona, where we live, at 4,600 feet elevation. Out here, it's all about the elevation.

I think of my friend Benny, who has hiked forty-six of Colorado's fifty-six 14,000-footers. He'd run up Humphrey's Peak before breakfast. If I can make it to Castle Rock, south of Denver, he's supposed to join me for a drive to the North Dakota Badlands.

At least the car is running fine. It's a bone-white 2015 Buick Enclave. My youngest daughter—Number 3 to you—nicknamed it *the Heat* because she wanted me to call her at school and say, "I'm coming to pick you up, and I'm bringing *the Heat*."

She must have gotten that off a cartoon, but it stuck.

My last gas-powered car, I reckon. A part of me hopes it dies on this journey, ideally in a way that gives me a payout from the insurance company.

It's on its second engine. The first died at the end of the 5,000-mile journey. Number 3 and I made to our cabin in Maine and back to Arizona. The engine stopped, and I barely got it off the road a hundred yards from our driveway. It seemed fitting that we had to walk the last leg of that epic journey. What memories I cherish from that trip with my third and final daughter... I would stay forever in those moments, if I could, cruising with my eleven-year-old without a care.

I crack a window, and the scent of pines drifts through the car. If it were later in the day, I would scan for elk, but I'm sure they're laying low on this bright afternoon. And as we get further from the mountains, the pine forest diminishes to prairie and then rugged desert. I know what's coming our way—at least regarding the landscape for the next five hundred miles—and I say a sad goodbye to the green.

We pass Cameron and its trading post and then cross the Little Colorado River.

I turn on the radio and find NPR, hoping for some news.

Instead, I get some guy talking about daylight savings. He's a Navajo—a guest—and apparently an expert on daylight savings.

He says, "Only the white man is dumb enough to think if he cuts a foot off one end of a blanket and sews it onto the other end, that he has a longer blanket."

I flip off the radio. Why does that bother me? Because I come from Arizona, where we don't practice daylight savings, but the Navajo Nation does—which seems a little hypocritical to me.

We continue in silence.

Soon, on our right is a painted landscape of rolling, multi-layered sand hills. Beyond that, the land stretches away to the far horizon, almost violent in its bleakness—Indian land. I know somewhere out there are the Hopi mesas. The San Francisco Peaks I passed earlier are sacred to the Hopi because their spiritual guardians and katsinas reside there for part of the year.

At this stage of the journey, Navajo and Hopi reservations seem more appealing than the harsh splendors of Lake Powell. And I don't think I could stomach the crowds at the Grand Canyon.

So, I turn right onto Route 160, a 180-mile "Scenic Byway" that runs from Arizona to Colorado. It passes the Four Corners about fifty miles after Kayenta and ends south of Ute Mountain at Cortez.

But I won't be going that far east.

No, I'm not ready for Colorado—especially Cortez. I'll continue north at Kayenta. After what I went through in Cortez with Bill… well, let's just say I'll never go near that place again.

A few miles down the road, I pass a sign that reads, "Dinosaur Tracks." I pull over and find an empty hut and a few chairs next to an open area littered with dinosaur prints. There are even a few areas, outlined by small stones, where whole dinosaur bodies have been fossilized into the rock.

I put Roman on his leash, walk him away from the fossils, and let him pee.

After, we look at the tracks again. There are prints everywhere! I see some—sharp-toed and deep—that I assume were from raptors, and others, wide and round, had to belong to something big and cumbersome. I wish there were a guide or someone knowledgeable here. One look at the sheer number of tracks makes me feel like I'm standing in what was once teaming with as much life as you'd now find in the African savanna — maybe more.

Soon, we're back on the road.

After ten miles, I slow as we drift through Tuba City, and one look around tells me I'm on the Navajo reservation — the largest res in the United States. Created in 1868, it covers over 27,000 square miles, spanning northwestern New Mexico, northeastern Arizona and southeastern Utah. You could fit Rhode Island, Delaware, Connecticut and New Jersey in it.

Tuba City has a population of less than 9,000, but like the rest of the Navajo Nation, it is growing.

On the outskirts of town, I pass a white kid standing by the road. He's skinny, his clothes hanging off him, and he wears a floppy cowboy hat. There's a saddle by his feet but no animal in sight. As I pass, he waves, hopefully, but I continue without slowing.

You might think it's rude not to pick him up, but I've got my reasons. I know who he is, which makes it extra impolite to pass him by, and I feel guilty. His name is Everett, and we've talked quite a few times, but for now, I must focus on driving.

Still, as I cruise along to the steady vibrations of the bad pavement, Everett's accomplishments play in my head. Everett has traveled the Southwest since he was seventeen. An old horse or donkey usually accompanies him, and you might spot him almost anywhere in Arizona, New Mexico, Utah or Colorado. He speaks a fair amount of the Navajo and Hopi languages, loves exploring the high desert and has a fascination for cliff dwellings.

For a young kid, he's had quite a few unique experiences: working on archaeological digs near Kayenta, traveling with a Navajo medicine man and helping with ceremonies, and working on Arizona ranches riding broncos and branding calves. He's also a talented artist and makes block prints and watercolors.

Additionally, he's one of the characters I mentioned earlier that I'd written about — the one who wanted to embrace the world.

All that adds up to someone who'd be an excellent traveling companion, but the main reason I don't stop for him is that he's been missing — presumed dead — for over ninety years.

Over the next hour, we pass small clusters of trailers and hogans at Tonalea, but I see no evidence of people away from the town, just far-off canyons and mesas. The flat ground is dull red and hard, the distant horizon low and shimmering in the heat.

It seems like anywhere you might want to go is far away.

I let the sweeping views of the plains and more-or-less empty wilderness pull me along. Yellow clumps of sage, tarweed and rabbit bush extend to the horizon.

And I know it's not really "empty." Twice, I glimpse jackrabbits scurrying for cover near the side of the road, and above me, two red-tailed hawks ride the thermals.

Still, it's hard to believe that over 330,000 people live here.

I drive along in a trance; Roman sleeps in the passenger seat.

Eventually, Black Mesa rises on the right, and I enter canyon country. The road curves along, following deep, twisting drainages on the left. They often turn away from the highway and disappear, diving into the wilderness.

I crane my neck and try to see more.

I know the Navajo National Monument is somewhere back there — probably six miles as the raven flies. If you followed one of those washes long enough, I'm sure you'd find a trail leading to it. There's a young boy in me who yearns to try to do just that... disappear into one of those hidden bends in search of a ruin.

It's definitely something Everett would have done.

The thought of adventure brings me out of my stupor.

And so does the moisture. You can feel it. As the walls of the canyons rise around me, I sense a coolness. I slow and roll down my window.

Roman sits up, shakes his head, and jumps up on the center console.

Flashes of green jump out of the hard crimson earth. I know that anywhere that gets shade and water will have creosote bushes, prickly pear cacti, yucca and sagebrush. Along the washes would be cottonwood trees and junipers, and if I came after the spring rains, I might glimpse a vast desert bouquet of wildflowers.

We pass Tsegi and its scattering of hogans. In the fertile valleys along the road, I glimpse horses and sheep. The animals and vegetation are a nice change.

Another break I get is the radio. I move the dial to 88.1 FM and am relieved to hear Hopi Public Radio KUYI come through loud and clear. It's a great station.

Today, they're playing some mellow blues, which suits me fine.

After Tsegi, we leave the canyons, and the land flattens again.

We continue on Route 160, which was put through in the 1950s. Sometimes, it's flat and straight as an arrow; other times, you roll up and down and feel like you're on a roller coaster. They didn't do a great job laying down the pavement, and the steady, rhythmic bumps during the flat sections remind me of being on a train.

Heavy rains and extreme weather have done their best to wear the highway down, too, and you've got to keep your eyes open for potholes. Roman is curled up in the passenger seat, not all that anxious to see what's causing the turbulence. Now and then, he opens one eye and stares at me, which is his way of protesting the constant vibration of the road.

There's little cell reception, and for most of the ride, I hope I don't break down in the harsh yet beautiful terrain. I glance at Roman again, and he must notice the nervousness in my eyes.

He asks, "You gonna freak out again?"

I shake my head. "I'm okay." I've stopped thinking about bills and responsibilities, but with the remoteness of this road, I'm now worried about being stranded. Climate Change has made life here even more challenging, with drier conditions resulting in droughts, more intense wildfires, and decreased water for livestock, crops, and people. Break down on the wrong, lonely stretch of road in this part of the country, and if you don't have enough water, you might become a statistic.

Roman stares forward defiantly. He can sense me tensing up.

He hops onto the center console and pretends to scan the horizon for his archenemy — the coyote. He already has no memory of crashing into the radio console a few short hours ago.

We call him a "rescue" because my wife found him online but was horrified at his living conditions when she drove down to Phoenix to pick him up. As a pup, he was owned by a pink-haired, aging stripper with a yard that looked like a recycling center. In the few minutes my wife was there, the woman yelled at everything — the dogs, the neighbors, the doorbell, etc. — and she couldn't wait to get him out of there.

As I mentioned, he's not the smartest critter, but he's all heart. He once flew to Maine and then rode with us as we drove back. I doubt he ever realized he was in the air or had crossed the country.

We're about an hour out of Kayenta when my mind begins to drift again. The road is straight and dull, with nothing to keep my attention, and before I know it, I'm dwelling on my issues again.

Money has always been a cause of my stress; there never seems to be enough, and I doubt there ever will be. There are also things left unsaid and other stuff I shouldn't have said at all. I feel like I abandoned my mom in the end. I wasn't there when she passed. I abandoned my sister, too, if I'm being honest. If I wasn't so stubborn, we might have patched things up. Sometimes, I wish I could abandon myself. But I'm tough to ditch.

I glance in the rear-view mirror again and see someone sitting in the back passenger seat. I almost slam on the brakes but resist at the last minute when I see it's Everett.

Roman never realizes he just dodged a bullet as he continues to scan the horizon casually.

Everett is scribbling in a notebook and barely looks up.

"Thanks for the lift," he says with a smile. "It was getting hot out there."

Everett Ruess was born in 1914 in Oakland, California. His father was a minister, his mother an artist, and their combined influences sent him to Kayenta when he was only seventeen.

Nobody knows why he picked that desolate part of the country; it was before movies were filmed there, and few people knew about Monument Valley in those days. If you'd asked anyone about it, they would have said, "Why go there? There's nothing out there — nothing."

But that's precisely why he went.

And he saw a beauty most people didn't — or maybe couldn't.

I'm envious; he had a chance to explore something I never did — the old world. I've sensed it, maybe felt its echoes a few times, but most of it was gone by the eighties when I began to travel.

I feel empty thinking about how cool it would have been to drift around this area in the early thirties. During the depression, the reservations saw almost no tourism, and you would have the place to yourself.

Well, you and all the people who'd been forcibly moved there.

But Everett had his reasons. He wasn't religious, yet he felt when he was alone in the wilderness that there was an awareness there that he could sense — and that it could sense him.

He wrote hundreds of letters that his parents eventually collected and published in a book called *On Desert Trails*. His story, along with Christopher McCandless's, was related briefly in Jon Krakauer's 1996 book *Into the Wild*. He's also mentioned in Edward Abbey's 1968 book *Desert Solitaire*.

My eyes keep drifting to him, sitting in the back. He looks like he doesn't have a care in the world, except when his eyebrows scrunch up as he chooses a word or phrase.

"How does this sound?" he asks.

I live by the love of beauty and adventure,
and would be content to wander forever
in the wilderness.

I pause, then ask, "You think you'll wander forever?"

He shrugs, "Why not?"

"I don't know," I say, "the older I get, the more I feel I should have more stability. I used to wing it,' but I've got kids now — and responsibilities."

He laughs, and his voice's light, unstressed timber almost brings tears to my eyes. He flips through his journal, finds another verse, and reads it out loud.

I like the mysteriousness of life and the instability of things, and the uncertainty of the future.

Now I laugh. "Aren't we a couple of opposites," I say.

He grins from the back seat. "Maybe I'll rub off on you."

Roman glances in the back and then gives me a confused look.

A rock in the road turns out to be a large desert tortoise, slowly ambling across the hot pavement. I decelerate and swerve to avoid it, and when I look back into the rearview mirror, Everett is gone.

I see these apparitions regularly, although I don't discuss them with others. I think of them as spirits or ghosts, depending on the situation. It's better than thinking I have multiple personalities.

They're just voices that will not be ignored.

There are past travelers, friends, and even a few family members. Twenty-four of them, by my latest count. A bunch are authors, and a few are musicians, too — although they, thank the Gods, only quote lyrics.

Last year, to escape my troubled mind, I made a list of books by American authors who had taken road trips on US soil. I called it *The American Literary Nomad's Reading List*. Ultimately, these authors also became more voices in my head, constantly trying to offer advice or relevant quotes.

They all sit behind me, speaking up when the situation arises. I'd love to ignore them, but they know me too well. They know my triggers and are experts at finding the chinks in my armor.

A sign appears, informing me we're only a few miles from Kayenta.

I drive through Kayenta, and I'm tempted to get a room. For an old guy not used to driving, it's been a long day — 3 hours, roughly 179 miles — and I could shower, but I'm still reluctant to mix with people. I glance at the sun and am surprised at how late in the day it is. Where did the time go? When I was younger, I would knock out five hundred miles daily without breaking a sweat, but not now.

There's also Roman to consider. Not every place will allow dogs, even awesome ones like my companion, and I just can't be bothered to research and find out the best deal or which ones allow pets. Honestly, I'd most likely sneak him in, but it's best to know when you're breaking the rules.

I'm tempted to check out the Wetherill Inn because its namesake, John Wetherill, had contact with two people I'm slightly obsessed with: Everett Ruess and Theodore Roosevelt.

Roosevelt came to Kayenta in 1913, four years after his presidency ended, when he was fifty-four. John Wetherill, a southwestern trader and explorer credited with "rediscovering" the Betatakin ruins and the world's largest stone arch, Rainbow Bridge, guided him in the area. I say rediscovered because Native Americans had long known about both locations, and Wetherill found them by following directions he'd been given by Navajo friends.

My cabin in Maine also has some Theodore Roosevelt history, but we'll get to that later.

Everett Ruess passed through Kayenta for the first time in 1930 when he was sixteen. Wetherill was sixty-four by then and only reluctantly gave Ruess directions as to where he might explore because he feared the young man might die out in the wilderness.

A fear that very well may have been justified.

But all that history still isn't enough to lift my dark mood, so I continue through town, only stopping for a minute at a grocery store to pick up some bacon and eggs for tomorrow's breakfast.

Outside the store, a woman sells fry bread and Navajo tacos. I grab a few tacos for my dinner and share one with Roman. As to be expected, he gobbles his half down in a quick second. I suddenly realize I don't have any dog food and go back into the store to grab a bag—I can't keep feeding him what I'm eating.

I pull over about a dozen miles from town, just north of Agathla Peak—a towering volcanic plug that rises 1,500 feet above the surrounding plain. A dirt track runs off the road, and I follow it slowly until I drop into a shaded gully. I can still see Agathla, its peak casting a long shadow to the east. I park in a thicket of junipers that hide *the Heat* from prying eyes.

I know it's illegal for me to be here, but I'm suddenly overcome with exhaustion and need a nap. The two back seats are already folded forward, so there's plenty of room in the back of the Buick.

I crawl back there, intending to rest for a while before getting back on the road. Through the back window, I stare at Agathla Rock. The volcanic monument is sacred to the Navajo, and foreigners are not allowed to climb it. But in the early 30s, when Everett Ruess passed through the area, it wasn't forbidden, and one stormy evening, the young white man ascended it.

I have no intention of trying to scale the intimidating structure. I'm sure parking where I am is illegal enough, but it's late in the day, and my car is entirely out of sight in the brush. I figure I'll get some shuteye and then do some night driving.

Roman joins me and spins in at least a dozen circles before settling down. I'm more exhausted than I'd realized, and within minutes, I sleep like the dead.

Hours later, I wake to a movement. Something has bumped into the Buick, and I slowly look around.

On the hood sits a bobcat. It's of good size—I'd guess about fifteen pounds—with greyish-brown fur, almond-shaped eyes and pointed ears. There's no moon tonight, but the vast night sky of stars clearly lights the feline. The dog sleeps by my side, clueless.

I prop myself up and watch it until I am overcome by sleep.

There'll be no night driving tonight.

Later, I'm awakened again by the same movement of the car, like someone has just sat on the hood. I look around and see no bobcat this time. Did I dream it?

There's a slight glow to the east, but sunrise is still far off. I know I won't sleep anymore, so I pull on my jeans and socks and stuff my feet into my boots.

I step outside to pee and stare up at Agathla, trying to discern which route I would use to climb it. These days, it's age more than laws that prevent me from scaling mountains, but I still daydream about it.

Everett did the same thing, although he was usually trying to access the old ruins perched near the top of vertical cliffs. The ancient ones created barely discernable climbing routes called Moki trails, and Ruess excelled at climbing them—usually without ropes.

When he climbed Agathla Rock for the first time, a storm was approaching, and he wrote a poem about it called Pledge to the Wind while ascending. I let one of the verses wash over me as I peer through the gloomy light at the peak.

Onward from vast uncharted spaces,
Forward through timeless voids,
Into all of us surges and races
The measureless might of the wind.

I think of him, at sixteen, far from any family or friends, clinging to the rock before me. He never felt alone in the wilderness, although he eventually made Navajo and Hopi friends. They nicknamed him Picture Man. To them, he was an enigma.

They'd come across him, miles from any road, painting images of the Southwest. He was an emotional kid; sometimes, they could tell he'd been crying while painting.

They thought him a mystic and allowed him into their lives, and through that generosity, he saw a world that few have glimpsed since everything got so fast and busy. He was most likely among the last whites allowed into the Hopi kivas.

I think of the last lines in that poem and wish I had dared to declare something bold like that to the Gods—something more than just screaming. To shout at the heavens like Odysseus, announcing my intention to do battle. Everett did just that.

Here in the utter stillness,
High on a lonely cliff-ledge,
Where the air is trembling with lightning,
I have given the wind my pledge.

For such a sensitive kid, he had a set of balls on him.

Over the next hour, I lay in the back of the Buick and listen to the bush around me waken. The day begins with the soft cooing of a mourning dove, followed by a pair of horned larks singing their morning song from within a cluster of tamarisk bushes. Soon after, a family of Gamble's quail trot by, single file, their top knot feathers bobbing.

The horizon begins to glow orange, and over the coming moments, it burns yellow. I wish I dared to sing the Navajo greeting for Dawn Boy, as Everett might have.

Let beauty walk before me.
Let beauty walk behind me.
Let beauty walk all around me.

Instead, I find myself sobbing, not sure why I feel such loss.

I climb into the front seat and start up the Buick. Roman shakes himself, and when I open the door, he jumps over me and heads for a bush.

While he picks a spot, I pour water into a plastic bowl I set on the ground near the door.

He laps it up and then climbs back in. I empty the excess out of the bowl and fill it with a handful of his dog food.

When I set the bowl on the passenger seat, he stares at it with an expression that says, "What? No hot dogs this morning?"

I drive out of the gully, and soon, I'm back on the open plain again. All that life I awoke to is now hidden from me, and the world breaks into a stark reality of rock and dry scrub as the diamond glint of the sun leaps over the horizon, lighting the day.

We cruise along through Monument Valley and are greeted with a vast panorama. The monuments are far off but still look massive. The upper cliffs are dark red sandstone that sit on a broad shale base. The sand on the ground is soft and orange-red—I'm certain Everett would have called it vermilion.

I pass Michelle Butte on my right but don't get very close to any other buttes until we've crossed into Utah. Then I am surrounded: first Sentinel Mesa on my right, Eagle Mesa on my left, and then in rapid succession—Bear and Rabbit Summit, King-on-his-Throne, and Brigham's Tomb.

The road straightens out after that—aligned almost perfectly east-west—and after a few minutes, I pull over at what is known as Forrest Gump Point. This isn't a great time of the day to be driving east with the sharp yellow rays coming straight through my windshield, so I will stop until the sun is higher in the sky.

In the 1994 film, Gump ends his epic run here, with Monument Valley as a backdrop.

I pull over on a level spot with a view and cut the engine. It's early in the day, but still, people stop and take photos. I watch them for a few minutes before getting out. There's a morbid fascination: each new tourist scans left and right and then stands in the middle of the road while their companion takes a photo with a cell phone. Meanwhile, a few cars pass; all the ones moving east have drivers squinting into the sun, barely able to see. It seems like a pretty good scenario for someone to get hit.

I pop the trunk and rummage around for my cooking gear. In a few minutes, I've got my two-burner propane stove going, with a frying pan on it, heating up.

I set my kitchen on the south side of the car, where I can enjoy the expansive view without being buzzed by the passing traffic.

Although the sun still hits me from the left, the rays are delightful at this early hour of the day—now that I'm not driving into them.

"We're gonna start the day with an Edward Abbey breakfast," I say to Roman as I dump the pound of bacon into the frying pan. He eyeballs it and says, "Did you say bacon?"

The last of the tourists leave, and for a few minutes, there's no traffic at all. The only sounds are the crunch of sandy gravel under my feet and the bacon popping.

For a moment, I sit with myself.

When the bacon is done, I set it aside, crack six eggs and dump them onto the grease. Abbey always made this sound like the most sensible thing to do in the wilderness, but I'm sure I'll pay for it later.

I haven't seen Everett since yesterday outside of Kayenta, when he appeared in my back seat, and I doubt I'll see him today. He's in his element here—his happy place—so why would he want to spend time with a sad sap like me?

Everett disappeared in November of 1934, about four months before his twenty-first birthday. Shortly before he left Escalante, Utah, he sent off a batch of letters saying he might be out of touch for a few months.

In the letter to his brother, Waldo, he wrote,

... as to when I revisit civilization, it will not be soon. I have not tired of the wilderness... It is enough that I am surrounded by beauty...

And there it is again, that love of beauty. I let my eyes drift over Monument Valley in all its splendor. He's out there, I can feel it, and I wonder: is it enough that Everett experienced this, and that led me here? Or that he moved me—his travels and the words they inspired—and, in turn, I tried to inspire you, the reader?

I watch two golden eagles ride the thermals across the valley, their shadows dancing on the ground below them. Perhaps my favorite poem by Everett is entitled *Wilderness Song*.

Here are a few lines:

> *I have been one who loved the wilderness*
> *Swaggered and softly crept among the mountain peaks*
> *I have listened long to the sea's brave music,*
> *I have sung my songs above the shriek of desert winds.*

When Everett's uncollected mail began returning from post offices across the Southwest, his parents started organizing search parties. Because of the vast distances he traveled, it was—at the time—the biggest manhunt in American history. His last camp was located on the north side of Davis Gulch, a canyon of the Escalante River, and his two donkeys were still there, alive, in a small corral he'd created.

But other than that, they only found inscriptions he'd made in several places to mark his passing: NEMO 1934. He called himself Nemo either because he loved Captain Nemo and Jules Verne or because it was Latin for No Man or No One, and he was trying to shake his old identity.

Nobody knows; there was never a chance to ask him because he was never seen again—and no one ever found a NEMO 1935.

There are a dozen books and a dozen documentaries that all try to persuade the reader to follow one theory or another about what happened to Everett. Some think he drowned trying to cross the Escalante River, fell from some ruin he was trying to access, or was snakebitten. Others believe it was foul play and that an Indian or cattle rustler killed him. And still, others think the Navajo hid him away and that he grew old and died with them.

But nobody ever found his body, so it's all speculation.

The rising waters of Lake Powell buried Davies Canyon, where his last camp was located. However, I've heard recently that drought has dropped the lake so much that the old camp might have resurfaced.

I prefer to think he's still out there, somehow, ninety years later. I read his words, and I can't conceive that he is gone.

> *Say that I was tired and weary,*
> *Burned and blinded by the desert sun,*
> *Footsore, thirsty sick with strange diseases,*
> *Lonely, and wet and cold,*
> *But that I kept my dream.*

I can feel his spirit here, although I've got no way to convince you. I also have no way to persuade you of the value of someone having lived the life he did. How can you put a dollar value on the life of some kid who seemed a cross between young versions of John Muir and Walt Whitman?

It seems like I just have to hold onto his words.

In that same final letter to his brother, he wrote:

> *This had been a full, rich year.*
> *I have left no strange or delightful thing undone*
> *that I wanted to do.*

Maybe that's enough. Perhaps that's what I should do… shake off the tears, take a deep breath, and ensure this is a year in which I leave nothing important undone.

It's a challenging task at this late stage of the game, but I will try. I pack up my kitchen, load everything in the car, and head northeast across the dry, high-desert plains.

Agathla Rock, near Kayenta, Arizona.

Edward Abbey
(1927-1989)

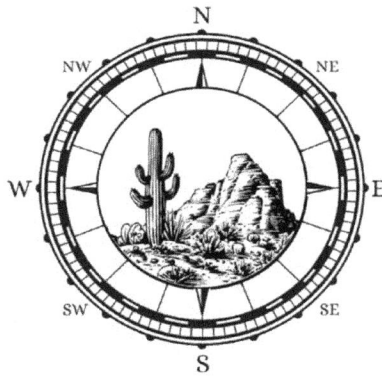

Double Arch, Arches National Park, Utah.

Chapter Three

UTAH

*I*t'll take us at least three hours to drive to Moab, and for most of it, we'll be passing through some of the most desolate yet fantastic landscapes in America. I'd guess it's about one hundred and seventy miles, but it feels more like I'm traveling back in time to the Jurassic than to some destination.

Roman settles down in the passenger seat. I set the cruise control at five over the limit, then put on KUYI radio and listen to the weather forecast.

Unseasonably warm temperatures will continue…

We skirt along the San Juan River, then the town of Mexican Hat, and soon after, the balancing rock the town is named after. I notice a sign for a road leading to the Valley of the Gods and can only imagine what geological wonders are hiding there.

I'd love to explore it, but it's a dirt road, and I don't want to take any chances with the Buick when it's already making time and driving fine. I hear Number 3 say, "Gotta take care of *the Heat*."

It's also looking close to post-apocalyptic out there, with that ruthless southwestern sun baking everything and barely a scrap of shade. The land has dried out, seemingly before my eyes, even though it's been going on for millions of years. The flat orange rock and sand are a shade darker here—redder. Tarweed, sage, Mormon tea and rabbit bush extend to the horizon, or the edge of the mesas, where the land drops into deep canyons.

In shaded areas, clusters of junipers stand defiantly.

In the distance are more lava plugs, like Agathla Rock. They tower over the plains like ominous sentinels. There are over eight hundred volcanoes in this area. Some are old lava domes, rounded and ancient, some are rugged mountains missing their tops, and others are cinder cones surrounded by ash.

The further west, the older they are.

Then, the land slopes downward for the next few miles. We pass uplifted bands of purple and white sandstone. I try to grasp what made them so wavey or how they got their color, but it's all too much to process. As I drive along, the terms rattle in my head: sedimentary striations, petrified ash, mudstone, white slick rock from the Permian extinction, or mud deposited on a layered seabed.

You can tell me that a specific layer was created in the Carboniferous period when ten-foot-long millipedes roamed the earth with giant spiders and dragonflies, but it's too long ago to make sense in my head. Who can imagine sixty million years ago unless you're watching a movie?

Still, now and then, I find myself cruising along, and suddenly, I can see it—I can imagine us driving along on the floor of an ancient sea with coastal dunes on our sides. I imagine a mosasaur cruising alongside us—or maybe a raptor on the shore observing our passing.

And I feel like a kid again. I hear Edward Abbey in my head, talking about the wonders of experiencing nature…

For a little while, we are again able to see, as the child sees, a world of marvels. For a few moments, we are able to see and touch and hear mysterious things-in-themselves. This is the most strange and daring of all adventures.

We drop off the plateau, and the road runs along a massive sandstone cliff — sheer for what I'm guessing is about four hundred feet. The sun has burnt the surface and is covered by a black patina — desert varnish. This sandstone was laid down in the late Jurassic. I wonder what tracks or fossilized dinosaur bodies are hiding in the rock. I imagine them watching through the cracks.

The road follows the San Juan River — flowing strongly for this time of year — for a bit before passing through the town of Bluff. From here, it's still a hundred miles or so. I've lost the radio, so I cruise along thinking about Edward Abbey for a while.

Abbey was an environmental activist known for advocating environmental issues and criticizing public land policies. He was born in Pennsylvania in 1927 and died in Tucson in 1989 at 62. He published twenty-three books in his lifetime, three of which greatly influenced me.

Desert Solitaire is a collection of vignettes about life in the wilderness, the nature of the desert, and his time as a ranger at Arches National Park. It's credited as a critical source of inspiration for the environmental movement in the 1960s.

The Monkey Wrench Gang tells the story of environmental activists fighting against the industrialization of the Southwest. It's been billed as "a classic comic gem of destructive mayhem and outrageous civil disobedience."

My favorite Abbey novel, *The Fool's Progress*, is a semi-autobiographical account of his journey from Arizona to his family farm in Appalachia. In the story, Abbey completes the drive in a broken-down truck with his dying dog. *The Heat* is still doing fine, and Roman isn't dying, but I still occasionally feel some parallels with that story.

I don't see Abbey often, but I hear him from time to time. We pass through White Mesa, and then Blanding, and his words drift before me.

Wilderness is not a luxury but a necessity of the human spirit, and as vital to our lives as water and good bread.

I glance at Roman, sleeping. He's snuck over by me and has his head on my lap. I can hear Abbey chuckling as he says,

When a man's best friend is his dog, that dog has a problem.

The land becomes even drier and more desolate. The clumps of green snakeweed turn yellow. Grey rocks and lifeless mounds of earth piled on top of red cliffs turn it all into a lunar landscape. Occasional spires and buttes burst out of the nothingness. I feel like I'm driving through Elliot's *Wasteland*, but I can't find any verses from that epic poem in my tired mind. I wish I had someone to spot me on some of the driving.

We pass the turn-off to the Hovenweep ruins, and a three-foot tumbleweed bounces off my windshield.

More bleakness. Knowing the names of some of the layers makes it even more confusing for me. I stare at pale White Rim sandstone-capped spires and mesas of Organ Rock shale and Cedar Mesa sandstone.

I'll stick with the sage and the tumbleweeds. Things I know.

My dad always talked about an old western movie where a cowboy kept finding love letters some woman was sending off into the wind, tied to tumbleweeds.

Suddenly, I wish I checked the one that hit me for a note.

North of us and extending to the west are the Abajo, or Blue Mountains. They peak out at 11,360 feet and look impressive as they tower over the rugged plains.

At Monticello, we pass them and now see a more significant range just slightly east of north. This is the La Sal Range, with a dozen peaks of about 12,000 and a highest elevation of 12,721. It sits to the east of Moab. They're too far away to examine which way one might summit, but I still daydream as they grow larger.

Eventually, the distant volcanoes and rolling plains bordered by rocky canyons give way to grass-covered prairies and small clusters of pines—and then, as we near Spanish Valley, a forest begins to take root.

There are big pines here, and the ponderosas remind me of Flagstaff. We pass a reservoir and start to see small farms. It's lush here for a while.

Suddenly, I'm in such a good mood that I begin humming.

I feel like I've just crossed a wasteland—a beautiful one for sure—but still, I did something that would have been a formidable accomplishment in ancient times.

Roman jumps on board with my positive mood and hops on the console.

I pull into a station and fill up. There's a convenience store attached, and I step in and grab orange juice, hotdogs and a big can of beans.

"At least Roman will be happy tonight," I mumble as I make my way to the register. I know my wife would frown on hot dogs for a second meal, but we've got beans this time.

On my way through, I also grab a bag of chips.

"Will that be all?" asks the teenage male attendant with a purple streak in his hair. I glance at the liquor bottles on a rack behind him and say, "Add one of those small bottles of Jack Daniels."

Before we leave town, we drive over the Colorado River. Arches National Park Entrance is only a mile away, but in that distance, we leave all the green behind. We're back in canyon country.

We enter the park—free because of my senior pass—and drive along Arches National Park Road. To the southeast, the La Sal peaks look menacing, as they should only a dozen miles away.

It's a magical landscape, and as my eyes sweep the horizon, I see two distant arches, several buttes with long fins, and even a balanced rock. And between it all are a hundred pinnacles. It all seems to defy gravity—as if the stones here were allowed to "grow" longer for some reason.

The arches, spires and eroded monoliths found here are all part of an underground salt bed called the Paradox Formation. To me, that sounds like something straight out of Star Trek, but apparently, it was deposited about 300 million years ago — the Jurassic — when the seas that covered the area evaporated.

More importantly, the park is known for its shapes — that's why we're here. It's a playground of outlandish structures, and I find myself amused by the names of some of the rocks and arches as much as I am by their weird forms. We pass Courthouse Towers, The Three Gossips and The Tower of Babel. And then, after a series of petrified dunes and a massive structure called The Great Wall, we cautiously drive past The Phallus Pillar — a one-hundred-foot-tall tower the locals call Cock Rock.

I pull over and park at Balanced Rock. A huge rock is balanced vertically on top of a long pinnacle, only two hundred yards away. The spectacle defies gravity. I glance at it, but I'm more concerned with the land around its base. Not too far from here, Edward Abbey spent two years living in a trailer. I know the trailer is long gone, but I'm still trying to see it.

It's quiet — almost ghostly quiet. I know it's offseason, but it's getting close to sunset, the prettiest time here, I'd argue, and there's not another soul around. And this is a national park!

I let Roman out to pee. Since nobody is present, I skip the leash. He stares at me guiltily for a minute, then trots off unconcerned.

When he's done, we load back into the Buick and turn right onto Windows Road. It's two miles to the trailhead parking lot, and I'm there in minutes. Abbey made this trip at least once a day — on foot — when he was a park ranger. There were only a few dirt tracks in the park in those days; nothing paved.

And that's how Abbey wanted it to remain. In his writings, he always called for self-control and restraint, not just from destruction by developers but also from tourism.

Sunset is more than an hour away, and the sun still has a bite, but I'm too mesmerized by the arches all around me to sit in the shade. So, I grab a water bottle, put on a hat and sunglasses, and follow the trail to the Window Arches.

I bring Roman with me, now on a leash, as he doesn't always exhibit common sense on our walks. We proceed to the North and South Window Arches and then Turret Arch. I'm feeling the heat when we return to the car, but I continue, following a northbound trail to Double Arch instead of resting. It seems strange to stare at a ribbon of rock, over a hundred feet up, that stretches across the sky.

I gaze at it in wonder.

I feel so lucky to be here and still can't believe I'm alone. Out of a country of hundreds of millions, I'm astonished that more don't prioritize experiencing places like this.

Nearby are Ribbon Arch and Cover Arch. Arches everywhere — there are over two thousand known arches within the park's boundaries — although technically, it's tough to get an accurate count because it's an ongoing geological process, so some will collapse while others are formed.

I'm sure I won't be so lucky if I ever return here. There will be crowds, traffic, and other things that will surely annoy me. Abbey knew it, too. He hated the improvements — like paved roads — all the tourist cars that came with the new roads, all the litter and destruction. He hated words like "Modern" or "Accessibility."

I used to think he wanted too much, but then I remember Baxter State Park — now expanded to include Katahdin Woods and Waters National Monument — in northern Maine. Most of the land was donated on the condition that it always remains primitive: no paved roads, no motors on the lakes, no pets allowed, etc. People can still drive through, but most of the exploring is done on foot or by canoe.

I feel dizzy and step into the shade of a shaggy-bark juniper. Even with a hat on, the heavy sun is baking my brain.

I think of my cabin in Maine, just north of Baxter, and imagine it's nice and cool there right now. I sip some water and think of the wind blowing through the poplars along the stone wall behind the camp. In this dry heat, it feels far away.

I ruffle the hair on Roman's head and give him a sip of water.

It'll be dark soon, and we need to find a campsite tonight. I feel stiff after sleeping in the car and driving all day, so I reluctantly head back to the Buick.

I get lucky and find a BLM campground along the Colorado River. Like the park, it's mostly empty, and I quickly locate a site near the gurgling water. Behind us, a monstrous stone wall rises hundreds of feet; it is dark red, patina-covered sandstone, like the one outside Bluff, and something about it gives me chills.

While I set up the tent, the setting sun slides a shadow up the rock wall and is then snuffed out.

I open my cot and lay my sleeping bag on it, and instantly, Roman is on it, spinning in circles before—eventually—settling down. I turn on my camp light, which takes off a little of the ominous feeling I sensed earlier, but it seems that when darkness descends, the rumble of the water gets louder.

Before I do anything else, I grab the Jack Daniels and pour myself a drink. Well, not exactly. I don't have any ice or mixer— other than the orange juice, which won't work—and I'm not even sure where my cup is, so I swig some out of the bottle. By the time it's dark, I have the hot dogs sizzling in a pan, a pot with the beans beside it, and a little buzz going.

As you can imagine, Roman watches the hot dogs cook intently from his place on the cot.

Later, the food is done—and so is a third of the whiskey. It's a small bottle—pint-sized, only holding a dozen shots—but still much more than I can, or should, try to handle in one night. We've eaten our share of hot dogs and beans, and I've put the rest in a plastic container. I don't have a fridge or cooler, but the dogs will last until tomorrow—and Roman would have been horrified if I'd just thrown them away.

There's a sky full of stars somewhere, but the massive wall behind me blots out most of the heavens. While I'm cleaning up my stove and putting away the kitchen, my camp light dims, and just as I finish, it dies completely.

I'm restless even more now, sitting in the dark with that big wall looming over me like a giant. My head spins with thoughts that I should just let be. I rummage around and find a few pieces of wood left by a former camper. I take the paper trash I've collected in a bag and stick it under a piece of wood. Before long, I have a fire going on in the grill.

The air has cooled, and I put on a jacket. I remember a joint in a plastic container was in the pocket. I fish it out and glance at the label: *Bubba Kush.*

I light it and take a few tokes between sips of whiskey.

It doesn't take long before I'm cruising along.

Maybe it'll help me sleep, I think, ignoring the other voices in my head that say it will only make driving tomorrow more difficult.

At one point, I drift off, and when I raise my head, someone is sitting across from my fire. He's in his mid-forties, with dark hair and an unkempt beard—both mixed with streaks of grey.

One look at the defiant glint in the guy's eyes, and I know it's Abbey—the great desert anarchist himself. He grins as he says,

To die alone, on rock under sun at the brink of the unknown, like a wolf, like a great bird, seems to me very good fortune indeed.

"Who said anything about dying?" I ask.

He shakes his head and extends his hand over the fire. I think he wants to shake my hand, then see he's motioning for the whiskey bottle. I hand it over.

He takes a big swig, and then another, and hands it back.

"Would you rather I talked about government agencies or tourism gone off the rails?" he asks. "Or how about the dams they've created in the west? Shall we discuss their future?"

I look down at the fire and mumble, "No."

"Why? Are you afraid of being rebellious? Of breaking the rules? Do you know the damage these government institutions are doing to America?"

"I'm not on a mission to change the government," I say.
He slowly stares at me and says,

One man alone can be pretty dumb sometimes, but for real bona fide
stupidity, there ain't nothin' can beat teamwork.

"Look at how they've messed up the Indian lands," he adds, "not that they could do it themselves."

I've heard his rant on Native Americans and have no patience for it and tell him to shut up. "I'm not talking about Indians or Mexicans with you," I say, "And I don't live my life based on government regulations—I make my own rules."

He nods, looks me in the eye for a minute, and says, "Well, I guess we have that in common. But what did I ever say that makes you think I hate Indians?"

I sigh, "I just lean away from any kind of name-calling or stereotyping—or try to—and you seem to lean into it. When I was a kid, every joke or story I heard involved a chink, spic or negro. There were worse names, of course, and if it didn't involve someone ethnic, it was religion—a Catholic, a Muslim or a Jew."

He grins, "Doesn't that sound all-American?"

He motions for me to hand him the bottle again and says, "I like anyone who's up for a little monkey-wrenching. I don't care what their ethnicity is."

I stare at him, wavering on the other side of my dim fire, his eyes glittering at the potential of vandalism.

And I'm not surprised, either. Abbey believed it was necessary to stop environmentally destructive practices no matter the cost. Ecotage, he thought, was the only form of activism that would halt things like damming wild rivers, strip mining, and clear-cutting.

In *The Monkey Wrench Gang*, four characters band together to stop developers from destroying the southwestern environment. They particularly hate Glen Canyon Dam and plan to blow it up.

They attack abandoned bulldozers and trains and cause a heap of damage. I sympathize with their cause, but I don't think those methods would work today.

"Do you know how much trouble you would get into today for pulling those stunts?" I ask him. "Any idea how much time you'd do when they caught you?"

He grins. "Tell it to the old-growth forest."

I want to say more, but what good will it do? Abbey had his time. He inspired a generation of environmental activists, even if many mainstream conservation groups condemned him.

The real-life environmental group Earth First! is said to have been inspired by *The Monkey Wrench Gang*. They use direct action and civil disobedience to halt the progress of developers and loggers.

I say, "These days, Climate Change is a bigger threat than development."

He stares at me unblinkingly and doesn't act like he even heard me. Finally, he motions for the bottle again, and as I hand it over, I see it's nearly empty.

After he takes a swig, I ask him about Arches. That's the Abbey I know and love. The man who wrote *Desert Solitaire*, and although it's clear the author hated progress and encroachment, you could sense deeply that he loved the desert.

"You want something from the desert?" he asks. Then he cranes his head back so he can see the sliver of night sky and, after a long pause, says,

I wait. Now the night flows back, the mighty stillness embraces and includes me; I can see the stars again and the world of starlight. I am twenty miles or more from the nearest fellow human, but instead of loneliness, I feel loveliness. Loveliness and a quiet exultation.

I smile. That's what I needed to hear.

He nods. Ultimately, I imagine it was the part of himself he liked best—the desert dweller, the nomad.

He finishes the bottle on me and then knocks it on its side.

He looks over the night sky and then says,

In the evenings after work I sit at the table outside and watch the sky condensing in the form of twilight over the desert. I am alone but loneliness has passed like a shadow, has come and is gone.

I stand stiffly, walk over, pick up the bottle, and throw it in my trash bag. When I look back at the fire, he's gone.

The next morning—as to be expected—I'm a train wreck when I climb out of my sleeping bag. My head is throbbing, my eyes sore, and my body aches. Even the sound of the river is painful.

Roman eyes me wearily but then forgives everything when I add a chopped-up hot dog to his food.

"Don't worry," I say, "we're gonna lay off the booze for a while."

The sun shines on me as I pack up the tent, and my sweat smells like whiskey. The light reflecting off the Colorado River hurts my eyes when I look that way. I gulp down about a third of the orange juice and feel somewhat revitalized.

Soon, we're on the road again, driving north for about a half hour before picking up I-70 and heading east. I curse the rising sun, put down the visor and try to block it while sitting taller in the seat.

Once we're cruising, I think about the night before and my conversation with Abbey. Those memories are fogged by the whiskey and then jumbled even more due to the hangover, but still, I contemplate what his stance on sustainability might have been.

Although Climate Change wasn't an issue in Abbey's day, he did focus on the fact that humans needed to confront the truth about their impact on the planet. He would have been horrified at the loss of life and biodiversity we've experienced in the thirty-five years since his passing.

His writings highlight the importance of preserving the environment and wilderness. He was critical of human interference with nature and supported living sustainably before it was trendy.

It wasn't just that we needed to stop environmentally destructive practices, but also that we had to achieve a balance between our human needs and the preservation of the natural world—concepts that align perfectly with the idea of living sustainably.

I begin to relax and, at the same time, let Abbey go.

I think of Benny and decide it's time to hang with the living, but Abbey throws out one last quote before he fades completely.

The one thing better than solitude,
the only thing better than solitude,
is society.

Balancing Rock, Arches National Park, Utah.

Robert Pirsig and his 1966 Honda Super Hawk.
(1928 – 2017)

American Literary Nomads

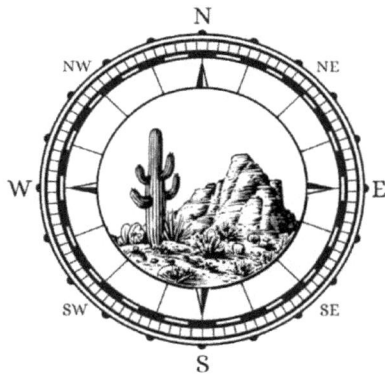

Entering the Rockies.

Chapter Four

COLORADO

*A*fter a while, the sun rises high enough that it's no longer in my eyes. It's a nice break as I'll be moving east for almost two hundred and fifty miles. I'm on a very impersonal six-lane highway now, but there are no other practical options.

The landscape is still stark desert, but I know I'll be in the mountains soon, and I can't wait. I'm yearning for coolness, shade and some altitude. I swig on the carton of orange juice until it's empty, still trying desperately to shake my hangover.

I'm also excited to see Benny. We went to high school together—Class of 82 —back in Hollis, New Hampshire! In our twenties, we painted houses together when summer found us back in our hometown, and we've kept in touch ever since. He was one of the few guys I knew who'd chased his dreams all over the planet: Belize, Costa Rica, Europe, Mexico, Fiji, Alaska, and Australia.

We also had a few authors in common, including Robert Pirsig and Joseph Campbell, and I'm looking forward to some good conversation. I've got tattered novels by each of them in my milkcrate full of books.

Robert Pirsig was born in Minnesota in 1928. His best-known work is *Zen and the Art of Motorcycle Maintenance,* which he published in 1974.

I thought Pirsig would be appropriate for this journey for several reasons. *Zen and the Art of Motorcycle Maintenance* is a deep, philosophical book that masquerades as a simple story about a father-and-son motorcycle trip. Their drive from Minneapolis to San Francisco is also a tour through Eastern and Western philosophical traditions, and we will share part of it — a 250-mile section of I-94 from Billings to Medora — with him on this journey.

Pirsig would have called this journey a *Chautauqua* — a type of narrated traveling road show — and I'm fine with that. My restless, chattering mind, these voices in my head, and my constant need to keep moving make me feel like a bit of a freakshow sometimes, anyway, and when I read Pirsig, I believe — for a few minutes at least — that I'm somewhat normal.

Here he is talking about life's direction.

You look at where you're going and where you are and it never makes sense, but then you look back at where you've been and a pattern seems to emerge.

And Joseph Campbell is just fun; he fits into any journey. He was an American writer and professor of literature who worked in comparative mythology and comparative religion. His work covers many aspects of the human experience.

When he was forty-five, he published *The Hero with a Thousand Faces* (1949), in which he discusses his theory of the journey of the archetypal hero shared by world mythologies. He coined the term "monomyth" to describe this shared experience.

He believed we were all on a "hero's journey" that only made sense when we looked at our lives in mythological terms. I'm down with that as well, although I don't know why it makes me feel better. Most of the heroes I know are in literature, and I suddenly imagine myself as Cervantes' Don Quixote, charging windmills with a lance.

I glance over a Roman, sitting quietly in the passenger seat, and say, "That makes you Sancho Panza."

That's not even close to what Campbell was talking about, but I still like the comparison. When Steinbeck wrote *Travels with Charley*, he named his modified truck Rocinante after Don Quixote's trusty steed.

Since the publication of *The Hero with a Thousand Faces*, various modern writers and artists have applied Campbell's theories to their productions. He gained recognition in Hollywood when George Lucas credited Campbell's work as influencing his Star Wars saga.

After a while, I see mountains rising ahead of me. I pull over at a rest area outside Grand Junction and let Roman pee, then again right before Mesa. At the second stop, I break out my stove and heat the unrefrigerated hot dogs and beans. They look fine, but I know my wife would be horrified.

Roman gives me a funny look that says, "Why are you so concerned with her?"

We continue, and I try my best to shut my brain down and just drive. I hear Pirsig trying to calm me down...

Sometimes it's a little better to travel than to arrive.

The truth is, I've been a mess since we crossed into Colorado. There's a ghost roaming this place that's been plaguing me for nearly forty years—way before any of the others.

It's that Bill guy again—the one I glimpsed in a suit eating a burrito back at the 7/11 in Flagstaff.

When I was twenty-one, I left home for the first time. I was gone a year and a half and managed to travel through forty countries. It was an incredible, pre-internet experience, marred only by the fact that I ran out of money after about three months.

So, I got creative, found work when I could and learned how to get by. I was scrappy and had a good sense of who to trust. I knew when to leave the party. I even came up with a list of *Rules for*

Survival—little sayings I collected that helped me get by. Things like: Don't chase the fire; Embrace the unknown; and Heed animal warnings. They might not mean much to you, but my rules saved my butt repeatedly when I was on the road.

Eventually, I disembarked an Air China flight in California and began hitchhiking across America to my family in New Hampshire. I had a few quarters that I had saved for an emergency collect call if I had to, but otherwise, I was broke.

Still, I felt certain I could make it.

My confidence knew no bounds in those days.

And that's why it threw me so when HE picked me up.

By the morning light, Bill looked like a boring, mid-Western businessman, but he changed throughout the day—and left a trail of destruction in our wake. Even after all these years, I still have nightmares.

He picked me up in Flagstaff at that 7/11, and eventually, I left him when I stole his car in Cortez. Even though that's on the bottom west of the state, I feel him everywhere in Colorado. Silly, I know… he could be anywhere… but Colorado is the last place I saw him.

Thank the Gods, Benny just wants to blast north with me, out of the state.

Jack Kerouac is the only author on my reading list connected with Colorado. He wasn't from there, but some of *On the Road* takes place in Denver. Kerouac, along with William S. Burroughs and Allen Ginsberg, were key figures in the Beat Generation. These "Beatniks" were part of a literary and cultural movement from the late 1940s and 1950s that rejected mainstream values and sought to challenge conformity. They were known for their unconventional lifestyles, experimental writing styles, focus on individualism, and heightened awareness. They often congregated in coffeehouses and jazz clubs.

The Hippies emerged in the mid-1960s and concentrated more on social and political activism. Although Beatniks and Hippies promoted personal freedom and self-expression, they were distinct movements. Some considered Kerouac the "father of hippies," but he never liked the movement and considered himself firmly rooted in the Beat Generation.

During their day, more people were upset about the use of drugs than what these groups believed in. Both Beatniks and Hippies embraced the use of psychedelic drugs like LSD and psilocybin mushrooms. The Beatniks began with marijuana and moved on to LSD because they felt it could expand consciousness. The Hippies took the use of psychedelic drugs to a new level, believing they could transform both individuals and society.

I have no issues with drug use, Hippies, or the Beat Generation, just Kerouac and the things he seems to admire in *On the Road*. I can't tell you how much I dislike that book, but I added it as an example of how "not" to travel in America.

Here's an example:

> *What Neal was, simply, was tremendously excited with life, and though he was a con-man he was only conning because he wanted so much to live and also to get involved with people that would otherwise pay no attention to him.*

I don't give Kerouac much airtime, and I'm certainly not going to today while I feel Bill's shadow lurking over me, but I will say that being on the road—whether you are 21 or 61—does not mean you get to cheat, steal or do unethical things. The same rules apply as when you are home.

Just because you are desperate doesn't mean you get a license to become a scumbag. I always liked watching people under pressure—you get coal or diamonds. And believe it or not, I've found most people get their shit together when something terrible happens. It's mediocrity that kills us. Minor tragedies.

So, Kerouac can take a back seat with his tome of never-ending, stream-of-consciousness prose.

I search the radio and stumble on a John Denver song, which instantly sweeps away all this heavy stuff, leaving me Rocky Mountain High.

I dig out my vape pen and try to roll with it.

When he first came to the mountains, his life was far away,
on the road and hanging by a song. But the string's already broken,
and he doesn't really care, it keeps changing fast,
and it doesn't last for long.

Soon, I'm deep into the Rockies, steadily gaining elevation. We're crossing the top of the state, moving east, and I feel myself putting distance between myself and Bill.

I pass mountains, many over 14,000 feet, and wonder which ones Benny has climbed. I think about him some more as the peaks slowly pass us by, trying to remember the names of his brothers-in-law who completed many of the ascents with him.

The names Michael and Dan float to the surface.

Benny earned a business degree at Keene State College in New Hampshire. He then moved to Colorado, where he worked as a ski instructor at the Crested Butte Mountain Ski School. There, he met the love of his life, Colette, and they were married in 1999.

Eventually, they had two boys, Alexander and Quinton. I wonder how old they'd be now. I've visited them all a few times in Colorado and envy the solid, happy life he created there.

The last time there, Benny drove me to a field where we sat and watched a small herd of bison. Benny said, "I just read about this herd. There are thirty-six bison, including two bulls, twenty females, and fourteen spring calves, living on 858 acres."

I grinned at his accurate numbers, and he smiled back.

"No, I literally read it this morning in the paper, and when I heard you were passing by, I thought it a good time to check out the herd. It's all part of conservation efforts by the state to restore bison to the land — and there are other, very cool, initiatives they're into here to help restore environments. It's one of the reasons I decided to settle in Colorado."

I watched one of the bulls approach. A wired fence separated us by about thirty feet. Across that distance, our eyes met: He looked defiant but humbled. I wondered if 858 acres were enough. Did he ponder that the way a human would? Obsessively… If only we had a few more acres. I hoped the Park and Game officials had a good handle on that number.

Benny added, "Used to be, when the herds got too big, they would cull a few and auction off the meat. Now, any surplus bison are donated to tribal nations as part of a program to return bison to indigenous lands."

We then talked about Theodore Roosevelt National Park in North Dakota and the large herd of bison that roam there. I had several reasons for visiting the area and was planning my visit. We watched the bull for a few more minutes. As Benny put the car in drive, he said, "If you ever head up there, give me a call. I'll take a ride with you."

After about four hours of driving, I begin to fade.

I was hoping to make it to Castle Rock and sleep in a real bed for a change, but that's not gonna happen. The highway slowly angles higher, climbing the Western Continental Divide until it plunges right into it with the Eisenhower Tunnel. It's the highest point on the Interstate System, with a maximum elevation of 11,158 feet.

Roman glances at me nervously as we enter the first of two tunnels, each a little over a mile and a half long.

As soon as we exit, I begin looking for a place to camp. I realize Benny is less than two hours away, but I'm drifting off and need a nap.

The sun is on the other side of the divide now, and I'm in shadow. It's about an hour from sunset, and I don't understand where the day has gone. It's like somewhere along the drive, I blanked out, and several hours skidded by. I did lose an hour by crossing time zones—but it's more than that.

While I set my tent up, a three-quarter waxing moon climbs over the horizon. I go to bed hungry, too tired to try to find a grocery store or diner. I fall asleep to the sound of crickets.

I awake later in the night. The moon is gone, and the insects are silent. I step outside to pee, and when I'm done, I scan the woods around me.

I see two figures on the edge of the forest, just beyond where I can make out details in the dusk. I peer at them, trying to make out details, although I know who they are. Everett and Abbey stare back at me, motionless and silent.

I know I won't see them again after this. They're Westerners, and I'm surprised they crossed the divide. It would have been nice if they'd waved or at least nodded, but instead, they simply disappear into the thick darkness and leave me alone.

Restless now, as a field mouse on a full moon, I creep back into my tent. I try not to think about Bill.

I'm up early, awakened by a grumbling stomach. I have a dreamlike memory from the night of waking up and checking my phone to find a message from Benny. Rather than drive to Castle Rock, he will meet me by the intersection of I-70 and Route 25, so we can get an early start.

The phone battery is low, and I discover I neglected to pack the charging cord. I shut the phone down and put it in the glovebox.

Roman gives me a stare that says, "Probably for the better."

I'm only on the road for an hour before I spot Benny on the onramp of 25, and before you know it, we're heading north.

I was looking forward to having another driver, but it turns out he had to pull an all-nighter to get the time off, and now he's knackered.

"Just let me take a little cat nap," he says as he climbs into the back and leans his head against the passenger-side window.

I glance at him back there, looking eerily like Everett.

"I thought you were retired," I say.

He laughs. "I was, but they pulled me back in—offered me a sweet part-time gig. It's only a few days a week, but when you said you wanted to spend more time up north, I knocked out some of next week's work, so I didn't have to rush back."

Soon, he's snoring. I pull into a Starbucks drive-thru, grab a coffee for myself, an extra for Benny, and a breakfast sandwich, and then begin driving north.

I'm a little let down. I was looking forward to talking with someone, and now I'm left alone—stuck in my head. I put on NPR and try catching up on the news, but the words pass through me, and I barely hear what they say.

Instead, I hear Pirsig again,

We're in such a hurry most of the time we never get much chance to talk. The result is a kind of endless day-to-day shallowness, a monotony that leaves a person wondering years later where all the time went, and sorry it's all gone.

The words do little to soothe me, and I focus on the road as we blaze our way North through Wyoming.

It's well over three hundred miles to I-90, my next destination, and I'll pass through Cheyenne, Casper and Buffalo to get there. I settle down and sip my coffee.

I look over at Roman and instead see Number 3 sitting there, smiling. "Shrek and Donkey, on the road again," she says.

I feel guilty that she's not really sitting there. Part of me wishes I'd taken her along on this mad road trip, but my mental state isn't the best these days, and I don't want her to see me like this.

My wife gave me the easy out by saying it was too much school for her to miss, but Number 3 didn't buy it, and when I left, she was angry with me for leaving her.

At Cheyenne, I see Highway 80 stretching west. About three hundred miles down that road is the Green River, which eventually feeds into the Colorado. In 1937, Buzz Holmstrom became the first whitewater river runner to float solo from Green River, Wyoming, to the Colorado River and through the Grand Canyon to the Hoover Dam. Several years later Buzz retraced Louis and Clark's expedition, but from west to east, which presented all sorts of challenges.

These feats, and many more, are recounted in *The Doing of the Thing: The Brief, Brilliant Whitewater Career of Buzz Holmstrom*, written by Welch, Conley and Dimock (2004).

I loved his gumption. At thirty-seven, Buzz was working in a gas station in Seattle, and he heard that nobody had ever done the length of the Colorado River — and took it as a challenge. His father had been a Norwegian and had taught him how to build boats, so Buzz built a small boat in his garage, towed it to Green River by himself, and set off on a fifty-two-day voyage that crossed 1,100 miles.

It's more of a river book than a road trip book, but I included it in my list anyway.

I know I have gotten more out of this trip by being alone than if a party was along as I have more time, especially at night, to listen and look and think and wonder about the natural wonders, rather than listen to talk of war, politics, and football scores.

Eventually, Benny wakes up. He sits there, rubbing his eyes and glances out the window.

"So, where the hell are we?" he asks.

I ponder for a few seconds and say, "I'd guess about fifty miles south of Buffalo."

"Damn, son, you've been making time," he says.

I laugh. "Just following my bliss."

"Right on," he says with a laugh. "That's the only way to travel — especially when you're on the hero's journey."

These are the first references to Joseph Campbell, and I feel my mood lighten. "Follow your Bliss" is one of Campbell's most quoted, most identifiable and arguably most misunderstood sayings.

As I mentioned earlier, Campbell felt we each walked through life on a hero's journey, and the mantra Follow your Bliss was a helpful guide—or even better, a compass—to help you keep on track. Campbell believed that the only way to ensure your life is the best for you is to chase after your joy.

My mom would have said the same thing but used the word *dream* instead of *bliss*. She is another reason I'm completing this road trip, but we'll get to that soon enough.

There's a bit of chaos as Benny climbs into the front seat, and Roman scrambles to the back. After, he takes a beat and watches the landscape pass by.

"Did you ever hear about Campbell's connection with the Grateful Dead?" he asks.

I shake my head, and he says, "Apparently, Campbell went to a Dead show in the mid-eighties and was blown away. I believe he said, 'Everyone has just lost themselves in everybody else here!'

"He met the band and became friends, and not long after, they put on a conference called "Ritual and Rapture from Dionysus to the Grateful Dead."

"I bet Jerry loved his philosophies," I say, "but I wonder how Campbell stumbled on the idea in the first place. It sounds like common sense these days, but people haven't always prioritized being happy or content with your life."

Benny nods and smiles, "I know this one—read it not too long ago. He got it from the Upanishads. He believed that Sanskrit was the world's great spiritual language, and he thought three terms represented the brink or 'the jumping-off place' to the ocean of transcendence—Sat-Chit-Ananda."

"That's pretty heavy," I say, pointing out the coffee I picked up for him sitting in the console. "It might not be too hot after all that snoozing."

He takes a sip, then grins. "Still warm—thanks!"

After another swig, he continues, "Okay, now bear with me. The word "Sat" means *being*. "Chit" means *consciousness*. "Ananda" means *bliss* or *rapture*. I'm not ready to put it all into my own words, so I will quote Campbell.

I thought, "I don't know whether my consciousness is proper consciousness or not; I don't know whether what I know of my being is my proper being or not; but I do know where my rapture is. So let me hang on to rapture, and that will bring me both my consciousness and my being." I think it worked.

We drive along in silence for a while, thinking about Bliss. Before long, we pass Sheridan, with the Bighorn Mountains on our left, and soon after cross into Montana. On our left is a sign for the Crow Reservation and soon, another for the Cheyenne Reservation on the right.

The land is very different from Utah or the Rockies, seemingly stretching beyond the horizon in an unbelievable flatness of prairie. At the same time, deep ravines, filled with lush growth, block access to the mountain ranges. We've been in the grasslands for a while, but we started in the drier shortgrass steppe and are now moving into the lusher northern mixed grasslands.

When we pass the Bighorns, the Pryor Mountains come into view behind them. Then the prairies take over again: western wheatgrass and buffalo grass mixed with colorful patches of purple coneflower and blue penstemon.

"I thought Campbell got all that stuff from Sigmund Freud and Carl Jung," I say out of the blue after about a half hour of silence. "Isn't his concept of myth related to Jungian dream interpretation?"

Benny nods. "It is, but even there, much of Jung's ideas about archetypes come from *The Tibetan Book of the Dead* and its deep fundamental insights into the human psyche."

I chuckle. "Look at us, a couple of Hollis boys out in the middle of nowhere talking philosophy."

He shakes his head, "Anything is better than talking politics these days."

The hypnotic lull of the horizon pulls us forward. We drift away from philosophy, the heavy thoughts too much for this late in the road trip and begin reminiscing about our high school days. I fade while Benny tells a story about his roommate in college, Chip.

While Benny rambles, I can feel Pirsig waking up. We're approaching I-94 and the portion of our road trip that will cross his motorcycle journey in *Zen and the Art of Motorcycle Maintenance*.

I glimpse him in the rearview: he's forty-six with a greying beard and head of hair. At first, he looks relatively normal, but closer inspection shows there's a lot going on in his eyes—and not all of it is good.

"You should be doing this ride on a motorcycle," he says, speaking over Benny as he tells a story.

"I know," I say and tell him to shut up.

Benny gives me a funny look and continues, "Remember that time we went to the 3-D theatre in Hudson and got thrown out because I got sick?"

I laugh, "You almost got us all arrested."

We joke about some antics on school trips to Spain and France in the eighties. Then we talk about our visits to his camp on Lake Winnipesaukee when we were only teenagers. A large bass lived by the end of the dock, and we'd sneak out there at first light and smoke with him. Benny named the fish Jake so we could "Have a wake and bake on the lake with Jake."

Pirsig gives me a look. I think he was hoping for a more stimulating conversation. Benny continues, telling stories—none of which I haven't heard—while Pirsig rolls his eyes.

He says,

When one person suffers from a delusion, it is called insanity. When many people suffer from a delusion, it is called a Religion.

"Not helping!" I say out loud, and even Roman gives me a strange look.

I try to deepen things and move away from recollections.

"Those were some great days," I say, "and I'm surprised we lived through half of it—but what about today? Are you happy?"

Benny sits there quietly, thinking, for so long that Pirsig restlessly throws out a quote.

The place to improve the world is first in one's own heart and head and hands, and then work outward from there.

I glare at Pirsig and tell him to chill out, and he settles down just as Benny finally answers my question.

"I think I'm as happy as I'm ever going to be," says Benny. "I'm loved, I've got passions and challenges in my life, and I really couldn't ask for more."

I sigh, more than a little jealous. "Good for you, man," I say.

By the time we reach I-94, we've traveled more than five hundred miles. I ask Benny if he wants to drive, and he shakes his head.

He says, "We can't make Medora today no matter how hard we push—it's over two hundred and fifty miles away—so let's camp and hit the road early tomorrow."

When we pass Bighorn, I pull off the highway and follow a dirt track that runs along the Yellowstone River. In a shaded riverbank, I pull up under a yellowing cottonwood and stare at the water.

Benny says, "Nobody around, gonna be dark soon. You should just crawl in the back of the car for the night and skip the tent."

He digs into his gear and pulls out a fishing pole.

"I'm gonna try my luck at catching us some breakfast."

As the sun begins to set, Benny walks off, and I'm left alone with my thoughts. I think I mentioned earlier how I wish I had Number 3 with me, but I also miss the others—especially Number 1 these days, as she lives in Hawaii, and I don't see her often.

Over the last few years, I made multiple trips to the northeast to be with my parents while they passed, and for much of it, I could tell Number 1 wished I was going west to see her.

Number 1's mind is the most like mine—poor thing. I get along great with the others; I relax more, and we have strong, loving connections, but somehow, I always know precisely where Number 1's mind is as soon as I see her. I always empathize with her—even when she doesn't want me to.

"Relax, Dad, I got this."

She's our adventurer. The traveler. The one who talks about her plans for years but doesn't mind just winging it when an adventure comes along. She's a high-liner, a freediver and a poet.

And she's fearless.

I thought with all my adventures, I'd be ready for the challenges and risks she takes. I did plenty of rock climbing in my youth, but I don't think I could walk across a high line with a five-hundred-foot drop underfoot.

Last year, she had my first grandbaby. They were checked into a hospital twenty minutes away in case of trouble, but instead, she delivered a beautiful baby girl in a big tub of rainwater in a small cabin in the jungle. Her name is Alcyone — she doesn't get a number because she is something new.

I wish Number 1 were here. I miss her. She might talk me off this ledge. She's used to dizzying heights. Exposure. I sense a great void before me, one I'm approaching rapidly. I think of her as I crawl into the back of the Buick.

I wonder if Benny had any luck fishing and where he might be now that the light is fading.

It's dark before I know it, and I fall asleep instantly. I am only awakened momentarily when Roman snuggles against my side.

"Good boy," I say with a sigh.

I awake in the morning to the sounds of Benny rummaging through my gear in the back. When I look up, I see he's loading things into the back of the Buick, not taking them out.

"Morning, Pardner!" he shouts cheerily, then points at the car's front end. "Your front seat was quite comfy."

I find it strange that I never heard him get in or out of the car.

He sets the cooking bin down, "And I found your kitchen — even got your stove going — when I realized you have no food. Nothing at all. What's up with that?"

Apparently, he didn't catch anything the night before.

"We'll have to get something along the way."

Roman hops out to pee, then dances around until I give him a treat. In this case, a small piece of mango.

"Who's a good boy?" I ask, and he gives me a doggie smile that says, "You fuckin' know who."

We're on the road in minutes, blazing our way east.

Benny and I ramble about our past as we push east on I-94. While we talk, the prairie slips away again. Now, broad stretches of the land we pass are cultivated. Still vast beyond comprehension, the horizon is now peppered with windmills, and long rolls of bailed hay occupy the foreground. The trees grow in rows — windbreaks — with no "forest" in sight.

Now and then, I spy a small pond with cattails and a dock and think about how idyllic it must be in the right season. But the closer we get to the Badlands, the more rugged the land becomes. We're approaching Theodore Roosevelt National Park, named after our 26th president, who first visited the area in 1883. The park covers over seventy thousand acres and is divided into North Unit, South Unit and the Elkhorn Ranch.

Theodore Roosevelt — or TR — has a lot of history here, and to be honest, I'm obsessed with some of it. In 1970, my father went to northern Maine and bought some land from a man whose grandfather had taught young Theodore Roosevelt to be an outdoorsman: William Wingate Sewall.

Growing up on "Sewall" land made me feel the ghost of young Roosevelt was around every corner — or maybe behind every stone wall. My first novel was a historical fiction account of his time in Aroostook County, Maine, entitled *The Making of Theodore Roosevelt*.

He may have cut his teeth in northern Maine, but TR's real challenges came when he went west to North Dakota — and when he went west, Sewall went with him.

I'd been warned that there is no food in the national park, so I stop at the Little Missouri Salon in Medora for a good meal before camping. The bar is decorated with memorabilia of cowboys and bull riding, and it looks a bit wild. However, it's early afternoon, and the place is mostly empty. As I lock the car, Benny says, "I gotta do some errands. Get me a burger and fries."

It's tempting to get a room at the Rough Rider hotel, which caters to Theodore Roosevelt and his North Dakota history, but I'm hungry for the wilderness and want to be outdoors.

I order two bacon cheeseburger and fry dinners—and two Heinekens. My head is spinning with the motions of the road. Vision sliding. The photographic bulls seem to be moving in my shaky stare.

By the time the food arrives, the first beer is long gone. I'm famished. I almost inhale my burger, washing it down with the beer I bought for Benny.

"Your loss, amigo," I say out loud as I look towards the door.

There's no sign of him.

Eventually, I order his burger to go. I pay my bill and leave, only to find him sitting in the Buick.

"What the hell?" I shout. "I've been waiting for you."

"Sorry, man," he apologizes, "I thought you got my text."

My battery is so low that I don't dare turn it on. I should address the issue and get my cell phone charged so I can get back in touch with the world.

Maybe talk to my wife…

But I'm not ready for any of that. I need to figure out some of this stuff on my own. Instead, I hand him his burger and get back in the Buick. Roman watches me wearily from the back seat, gloomy, until he snatches the few fries I'd set aside for him.

Before we enter the park, I fill up at the only gas station in town.

The convenience store where I pay is a busy little place. They have a monopoly on camping gear and snacks, and before I go halfway across the store, three different employees tell me there is a three percent fee if I don't pay cash.

I pick out a few over-priced cans of soup.

I ask about phone chargers and am relieved when they inform me they don't have any. Oh, well.

At the register, I grab another bottle of Jack Daniels despite half the voices in my head shouting that it is a bad idea.

We enter Theodore Roosevelt National Park and pay the thirty-dollar fee, which covers multiple entries for a week. The park is a beautiful mix of badlands, prairies, caprock, pillars and riverbeds. A few of the hoodoos reminded me of Arches, but this place is a whole different type of animal. As we arrive late in the day, I catch them mostly in shadow.

I follow the only road into the park, and after about five miles, I reach the Cottonwood campground.

The even-numbered sites are first-come, first-serve, and more than a few are open. The best time to see this place is the off-season, like back at Arches.

My tent site is nestled into a grove of cottonwoods. A path leads through the trees and emerges onto a prairie that extends for about five hundred yards to the bank of the Little Missouri River.

It's about a five-minute walk, and I stop and watch Benny move in that direction with his fishing pole. He gives me a smile that's tinged with sadness.

I fumble around in the back of the car. Take out the cooking gear. Eventually, I set up the tent.

Roman knows the ritual of camping now and watches approvingly. He steps closer when I set up my cot inside the tent, and as soon as I lay out my sleeping bag, he begins to spin in tight circles, trying to find some perfection.

I wished I'd counted how many times he circles before settling down, but he doesn't move once there.

An hour later, the sun is approaching the horizon. I take out the flask of whiskey but think better of it and stick it in my back pocket. I walk down to the riverbank. Benny is fly fishing, casting the line magically over the water. A beautiful array of colors fills the sky behind him, much of it reflecting off the water.

"You should come back—I'll cook up some soup," I say.

He shakes his head. "Think I'm gonna stay right here."

I glance at the sky. "It'll be dark soon."

He nods sadly. "You knew this would be a one-way trip for me."

My mind races as it tries to somehow hold back the truth. A truth that seems far from the reality of the last few days. I try again, seeing him as I last remembered him—alive in my mind—but the truth floods in.

He's not here—I've been spirit-walking with him.

Benny and I had talked about this road trip for a while, and he was supposed to accompany me, but then suddenly—after returning from a family diving vacation in Belize—he passed due to a cardiac arrhythmia.

I think of Colette and his sons, Alexander and Quinton, and feel guilty that their grief must be so much greater than mine. But they know how much everyone else loved him, too. It's hard to let go of good friends—and Benny was a unique and loveable guy.

Maybe it wasn't all just in my head, I think, as I watch his image flickering on the water. Maybe Benny played a part in some of this deception and camaraderie. I want to think so.

I do feel like we just took a long ride together.

Darkness is descending, and I feel empty without the light from the bright night sky. That will come, but for now, I'm left with only a lack of visibility.

I can still see Benny in the fading light, but soon he vanishes, and I'm left alone.

I find the bottle of Jack Daniels, twist it open and take a long pull.

Map 2: Medora, North Dakota to Chanute, Kansas.
(1,009 miles.)

Theodore Roosevelt, ready for the Badlands.
(1858 – 1919)

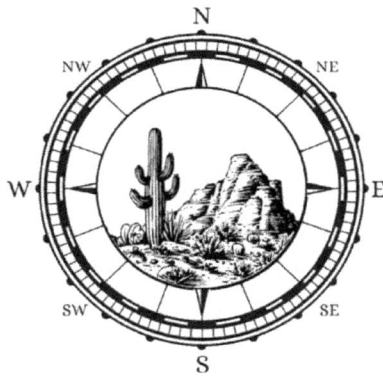

The Little Missouri River, North Dakota.

Chapter Five

NORTH DAKOTA

At the last minute, the sky flared with color — reds and maroons — that soon succumbed to nightfall but still felt like a sign. I sat on the bank of the Little Missouri, sipping whiskey.

I came here for a few reasons — you'll get an earful soon enough.

I'm not sure why it took so long. Seriously, this was my last state out of all fifty, and I just got here for the first time.

Roosevelt had his reasons, too.

He never owned an acre of North Dakota land; he squatted on lands belonging to either the NP Railroad or public land. But with an investment of $400, he purchased a ranch located thirty-five miles north of Medora, along the banks of the Little Missouri River.

In order to build a cabin and run the ranch, TR decided to bring out two Maine woodsmen — William Sewall and Wilmot Dow. Working alongside the men, he built the cabin in the fall and winter of 1884-1885. Compared to other cabins of the day, it was relatively luxurious.

Roosevelt loved the location and often reminisced about the shade of the cottonwoods or the breeze that blew over the veranda as he relaxed in his rocking chair. And you can sense his contentment in a few of his books, like *Ranch Life and the Hunting Trail* and *Hunting Trips of a Ranchman*.

I yearn to feel that contentment, but I'm too restless. Too wired.

I scan the prairie, surprised to find a luminous moon suspended above me. I somehow missed its rising.

I feel like it's watching me — like it knows about my failure on the medicine wheel. I swig on my bottle as I walk back and forth between my campsite and the river. Crickets and frogs sound out loudly by the water. The moon dims the stars, but I can still see the constellations and a few planets.

On one of my return visits, I grab my cell phone and stick it in my pocket. I also dig into my pack and fish out a joint.

Tranquil Elephantizer, sounds perfect.

I take a few hits, cough uncontrollably for a couple of minutes, and then choke down a swallow of Jack. Now we're cookin'.

There's a chill to the night, early fall, but I've been too preoccupied to start a fire.

Roman is in the tent, curled on the cot, deep in my sleeping bag. He's not going anywhere. He lifts his head as I enter the tent, looking worried.

"I got this," I say.

He stares back. "Bullshit."

Out on the prairie again, the moon has risen higher and seems less aware of me, but I still feel something haunting in the air. I've seen no sign of Benny and wonder if it's Roosevelt I'm sensing.

I try to think of the first time I heard of this place and his connection to it. I remember when I was fourteen, meeting a man who claimed his grandfather had been out here with TR.

That man — William Sewall — had taught young Theodore how to be a woodsman in northern Maine and, just as important, how to exist with the rough type of men who lived in the wilderness by taking him to logging camps. That had been when TR was twenty, and in those days, his biggest obstacle was getting over the death of his father and his own weak body.

When he came out west, he did so with a new spiritual weight that may well have defeated him. On Valentine's Day, 1884, both his mother and his wife, Alice, died in his New York City home.

His daughter, named Alice after her mother, survived her tragic birth, but he found he could barely be in the same room as her without bursting into tears because she had her mother's eyes.

In the letter he first sent to William Sewall, he ended his invitation to come out west with the words, "...so, as yet, the plan is doubtful."

But something happened during that first year that changed him; that gave him a momentum that propelled him through the rest of his life. Theodore came west to escape his past and instead stumbled into his future.

He was trying to move on, but progress was slow and painful. Both Sewall and Dow brought out their wives during that second winter, and to Theodore's dismay, both women became pregnant. When Alice passed, he swore he'd never have children again, and now he had to watch, restricted to a cabin in late winter, as they neared delivery.

And that's another reason why, in the spring of 1886, when someone stole his boat, he wasn't having it.

The weed and the Jack Daniels combine in my blood and send me reeling. I stagger back and forth across the prairie, angry and not exactly sure why. I think of my wife and the unresolved issues there, and of Benny and his untimely passing.

I'm getting myself worked up when my mother's face appears in my mind and calms me for a beat.

My mom, Pat, always talked about her visit to the Dakotas. One evening, while staying near a reservation, she went on a star-viewing tour. The native guides took everyone for a short drive to a hill, where they observed the night sky for about an hour.

When it was time to leave, Pat said she wanted to walk back. The man in charge didn't think it was a good idea and tried to talk her out of it. But when Pat had her mind set, getting her to alter her course was tough, and eventually, they left her.

She began to walk back. There was only one road, in the middle of nowhere, so she didn't think she could get lost, but in the end, it was close to four miles — not one as she'd thought.

It was around midnight, and there were no other cars except the van, which returned twice to try to find her. Each time, she hid in the brush and didn't come out even when she saw who it was.

Over the years, she talked about that long, solo walk back along the Dakota prairie while the stars glittered powerfully above her. She shared how she felt alone and afraid but also powerful and connected. Even in her final years, that night returned to her repeatedly, and I promised her someday that I would go there and see it for myself.

So here I am.

I take out my phone and almost turn it on, but instead, I stick it back in my pocket and take another pull off the near-empty bottle.

When I next reach the river, my anger bubbles to the surface. I stare at the wilderness surrounding me, the vast, wild Badlands that, even now, as a National Park, have hardly any people in them.

I gaze over the water as it sparkles in the moonlight. I think of the forty-six, fourteen-thousand-plus peaks Benny climbed and how he only had a few left. It seems so unfair that he's gone; I would have guessed he was one of the healthiest members of the class of '82. I even told him that!

Why does fate seem so random? People wonder why I get so mad when they talk about an all-powerful, all-knowing, loving God. I'm all for experiencing God — the Godhead, Nirvana... call it what you want. I've done that on mushrooms! — but please, somebody, show me the proof of a benevolent, active force making this world better.

Suddenly, I find myself shouting, "Benny!"

I glance around for a minute, but there's no reply or ghostly apparition. I am alone.

Now I just scream, my body shaking, until I'm hoarse. Then I huddle on the bank, feeling I've somehow offended the wilderness.

Or at least shocked it.

In a softer voice, I whisper, "Mom?"

There's no sign of her either. I'm not religious in any sense, and I don't believe in ghosts, but I still thought that coming here, I might feel their presence. I've sensed these two with me for a few days now, but there have been no signs that they are anything other than figments of my imagination.

And then, about thirty feet up the bank, I see a figure crouched down, peering at the water. It's not Benny or my mom, but instead Theodore Roosevelt, in his late twenties, wearing a buckskin outfit.

He motions for me to be quiet and nods at the river.

"He's out there," he says, "Red Finnegan and his two companions. He's on the water, and if it weren't for the darn ice, I'd have him by now."

I remember the story. One evening, a character named Red Finnegan was drinking in the town of Dickinson and offended someone. Red had a mop of red hair, a big red beard, and a buckskin outfit with many tassels.

Eventually, he passed out, and when he woke, he found all the hair on the left side of his head had been shaved off, including half the beard and even half the tassels on his buckskins.

He was so livid when he woke that he ran around for an hour, trying to shoot anyone he could. He fled with two others and was on the run when they stumbled upon Roosevelt's boat, which he thought might be a good getaway vehicle.

After all, who would be crazy enough to chase them down the Little Missouri River under winter conditions?

I knew who. It was the intense apparition before me, one whose eyes burned with purpose. Young Theodore Roosevelt had learned to be an outdoorsman in the same woods as our cabin in northern Maine, and I thought I knew him well, but the guy standing before me was a different man.

He was only six years older, yet his eyes were those of an old man. He looked stronger but tired at the same time. A weariness had a hold on him, and it was only his grim determination that kept him moving.

"So, you're going to hunt down a man for stealing your boat?" I asked.

He grinned as if accepting a challenge and said, "Not at all. There's already a bounty on Red, but I'm not chasing him for the money, either. His crime was lacking ideals."

I'm a little unsteady and sit on a fallen cottonwood trunk. "I didn't think that was a crime," I say.

He laughs. "Should be." Then he adds:

> *If a man does not have an ideal and try to live up to it,*
> *Then he becomes a mean, base and sordid creature,*
> *No matter how successful.*

Ready for an adventure that might divert his mind, TR had Sewall and Dow build a raft. Soon, they were on the river, flowing north, in an attempt to catch the thieves. About seventy-five miles later, they found them camped near the mouth of Cherry Creek.

Roosevelt takes a step closer and stares at me.

"This is no place for the weak," he says. "This is where you come to either live or die."

"Is that why you came here?" I ask.

He gives me a sad glance and flashes his teeth as he says, "I named my ranch Elkhorn because, on my first visit there, I found two elkhorns interlocked in a grizzly tale of the struggle for primacy. The males had been butting heads when their horns became locked and, unable to free themselves, had starved to death."

As I look over the water, I think of those elk, staring at each other over the coming days until one, and then the other, soon after, died.

"You can never quit," he says, then drops down the bank and follows the sandy shore downstream.

After they jumped and captured Red and the other two men, Sewall and Dow continued downstream with the boats to a location where they could return with a wagon.

With only a shotgun, Roosevelt marched the three men through the surrounding hills and onto the plains. Even when he borrowed a wagon, he let the three men ride while he walked behind them for fear that they might attack him if he was riding. Ultimately, he walked about seventy miles and went several days without sleep.

He collected the fifty-dollar reward in Dickinson, but what had changed inside him was worth far more.

I come to, later in the night, slumped against the log. The moon's position has changed; I've been here a while. I lay there listening to the cicadas and slowly remember a frantic call with Number 1, during which we talked about my state of mind.

I search for my phone and can't find it.

And then TR appears again, scaling the bank with a determined look. He glances at me, shakes his head, and stares at the water.

A pack of coyotes sings out from across the river. We listen to the crazy cacophony until it dies down. I expect him to ramble on about Red Finnegan, but instead, he says, "I lost my mother recently as well, you know."

I'm surprised he knows about my mother, but really shouldn't be, I guess. Pat passed two months before, so close to Benny that I can never remember who was first. One was one day ahead of the other.

"She was a southern belle, my mother," says Roosevelt. "Sweet and gracious. Her name was Martha, but everyone called her Mittie."

Before I can say anything, another pack of coyotes starts up, and this one is closer to us. Soon, the ones across the river answer back, and the night is alive with their beautiful calls.

TR doesn't appear to hear any of it. He stares at his feet as he says, "Typhoid took her before her time, just when I needed her."

I sit up and realize the small plastic bottle of Jack Daniels has been in my back pocket, poking me all this time. It's empty. I search for my phone again and instead find the joint and a lighter.

TR watches with an amused expression as I take a hit.

Eventually, I say, "Your mom died on the same night as Alice, right?"

His eyes flare as if surprised I would say her name out loud.

He shouts at me. "Sir, you are out of line!"

As he storms away, I turn into the indignant drunk and yell after him, "Tally Ho, motherfucker!"

I wake later to a gentle rain falling, hitting the prairie all around me with little whispers that say, *"Pat, pat, pat… pat, pat… pat, pat, pat…"* I laugh out loud.

"I am large, I contain multitudes…" I say and burst out crying again, but this time, it's tinged with happiness as I now feel my mother all around me. The kids at her daycare and her grandchildren called her Pat Pat, and I hear ten thousand little voices whisper *Pat Pat…*

I lift my head and see I'm far from the river or the campground, out on the prairie. The stars are sliding across the sky, between clouds now, and I realize I'm still drunk—or high—or both.

I tilt my head back and sink into the lush grass that's about a foot high. Elk begin bugling all around me, and their calls are otherworldly. The rain stops, and a wave of petrichor floats by.

I fade off and wake later as something large moves toward me, and there's more than one of them. I'm hidden well but can't see anything. I hope it's not bison—but what else could it be? I hear grazing and slow steps forward. It gets louder and louder. I hear grunting, snorts, and the clop of hooves.

I don't want to end up a statistic or comical news story.

I get ready to get up and run if I must. They sound only feet away, and I don't want to wait until they are upon me.

I sit up and look around.

I'm alone, not a man or animal within miles.

Then, TR appears again.

He's mad now. I can see it in his eyes.

"How dare you talk about my Alice when your house is hardly in order."

I guess it's not surprising that he also knows about my baggage. He's talking about an indiscretion on my part, one that embarrasses me deeply. I stare back at him, angry at myself as I remember the event.

A year ago, while grabbing a library book from my wife's nightstand, I glimpsed an open book. It was my wife's journal, and the words she'd just written shook me to the core.

They burned into my mind a message that our happiness was just an illusion. I'll jot them down below, and you can decide if I overreacted.

In Class, I think I actually glowed when I saw you and smiled.
Time froze, like a beat happened, outside of time.

Over the coming weeks, I became obsessed with finding out who this person was who had made my wife glow and feel alive. I began by casually asking her if someone else in her life had caught her eye—a yoga instructor or a musician, perhaps. We've been together thirty years, and I tried to be understanding and accepting if our love life had faltered.

But she only said there was nobody. She wasn't terribly happy in our relationship, she said if I wanted to know the truth, but there was nobody else.

I tried to believe her, but I had seen her words. I had to know who was this person that made her glow, that made her heart beat so.

I pushed and prodded, and our relationship got worse until finally, we began having serious talks about separating. When I thought all was lost, I admitted to reading her journal and knowing there was someone.

She laughed then and told me that in class, they'd been doing an exercise of looking at themselves in the mirror and trying to see their Inner Child.

And she had.

I was dumbfounded. "You were writing about seeing yourself? Your inner child?"

She nodded, and I felt double the fool. All that wasted energy and emotion. But worse was that I saw it as the end of us. If it had been another man—or woman—I might have embraced the competition. But how can one battle against a person trying to get to know themselves?

And now, replaying it all in my mind before TR's disapproving stare didn't help.

"Alice was my first wife and the true love of my life," he says. "She died two days after giving birth to our daughter. Our time together was short—we were only married for five years—but I loved her dearly. Most people know only Edith Carow, my wife during my presidency, and out of respect to her, I never mentioned Alice in public."

He looks along the river and adds, "The only tribute I ever wrote for Alice was penned at the Elkhorn Ranch. She would have liked it here—and when I'm here, I feel her presence."

I'm feeling nauseous, and the sky is spinning. I wonder if I'm going to get sick. I think of my anxiety and how it shaped our relationship. I'm the one that got lost. I can't pin it on anyone else.

The moon isn't visible anymore, and it's gloomy out, so I search my pockets for a lighter.

Instead, I find my phone.

I turn it on and see there's less than five percent battery.

I glance down, and there's a text from my wife. It reads,

I love you – call us when you can.

I've barely read the words when the phone shuts down. My mind does the same, and I pass out again.

I wake up sometime later when Roman slams into me.

"Arg!" I shout, and then when I realize it's him, "Good boy! Good boy!"

He's looking all around us, wide-eyed. What made him suddenly seek me out and leave the safety of the tent is beyond me, but I'm so glad he's here.

I stagger to my feet and start stumbling toward the campground. I'm doing my best not to look like Captain Jack Sparrow, although nobody is watching at this late hour.

"I'm okay," I tell Roman several times, and by the time I reach the tent, I'm starting to believe it.

Thankfully, he holds back any comments, and when I crawl into my sleeping bag, he's right beside me, spinning in circles until he reaches perfection. We both sigh before we fall asleep.

I sleep like the dead for a few hours, but in the silent pause before dawn, I wake to the coyotes singing again. The temperatures have dropped considerably in the night, and I wish I had brought a better sleeping bag.

I lay there, trying not to think too much about the night before. Roman helps warm me, but I'm not used to the cold and begin to shake. I attempt to quell it, but trying not to shiver when you are freezing is like trying not to be jealous when you are heartbroken. Like trying not to be nervous when you notice a cop following you and you've been speeding.

I keep an eye on the horizon, and as soon as I see the slightest glow, I grab a few things and make my way to the car. I figure I can drive through the park for a few hours and return later to break down the tent when the sun is up.

My teeth are chattering as I unlock the car.

Now is when I could use Number 2. I haven't talked about her yet, even though I love her just as dearly as her sisters. She's our healer... the calm child who relaxes me when I'm stressed. She's a manager at our spa in Sedona, and I'm not the only one who raves about her therapeutic abilities.

When she was young, she was my hiking companion for a few years. I called her my Sunrise Girl because she jumped right out of bed anytime I woke her up, asking to do an early-morning hike, regardless of when she went to bed or how well she slept.

She would have been up with me now, eager to explore the park. And I suspect she might also help me get out of my head and be in the moment—something I desperately need.

The heat is intoxicating as it restores my circulation.

I down the contents of my water bottle and refill it from a jug in the back. When I feel somewhat normal, I put *the Heat* in gear and start down the park road.

Usually, there is a thirty-six-mile loop through the park, but currently, it's closed halfway. You can still drive about fifteen miles, but then you return the same way. Along the drive are numerous pullouts, some with viewpoints and hikes.

I see no other cars as I follow along, marveling at the rugged outcrops of rocky ridges that skirt the river. A ghostly fog hovers above the water, and geese honk from within it.

The road turns into a gully, and I glimpse two mule deer moving through the shadows. One stops as if considering crossing the road but then stares at my car as I pass.

The sunrise takes forever and seems undefined. There's a soft haze over everything—smoke from fires in Canada—and the vast, endless sky glows orange. I'm tempted to ramble about Climate Change here, but after last night, the fight has left me.

Instead, I slowly drive deeper into the park, letting the views fill my mind instead of my normal chatter. I feel surprisingly relaxed today, like I've shed a great weight. My wife would say more self, less ego.

On another bend in the road, I pause as a flock of turkey gobbles its way across the road. I smile at them and make a gobbling sound at the last straggler. I'm slowly learning a few of the birds here, and in the morning coolness, I glimpse a western meadowlark and several grasshopper sparrows.

Over the next hour, I'm continuously encountering animals. On one straight section, several pronghorn skip alongside me as I drive, and then, in the field to the left, I spy five wild horses. I park and watch a young colt buck off some of its nervous energy.

At one pullout, a sign highlights the numerous burrows in the ground. It's too early to see any of the inhabitants, but later in the day, I see groundhogs, pocket gophers, and ground squirrels here.

On one of the short hikes, through a field of sunflowers, owl's clover and purple coneflower, I see a herd of bison in the distance. By the time I'm returning to the car, the day has heated the wheatgrass enough that the grasshoppers are up, and they explode with each footstep I take.

There's magic here. I can feel it.

When I reach the barricade indicating that the road is closed, I turn and head back. After its 'dark night of the soul,' my mind is clear now, and I know what I must do. I won't be returning to Sedona, at least not right away. I have to get a better grip on things if I hope to ever salvage my life. Or my marriage.

Instead, I'll continue east—all the way east—to the cabin in Maine. That's where I need to be right now. All this talk of Roosevelt and his ordeals makes me think of him as a younger man.

I need to return to the beginning, to where he first learned to stand independently.

Where we both did.

As I come over a ridge, I encounter a big herd of bison—maybe seventy animals. There seem to be mostly cows and calves, but a large bull stands facing the sun on a nearby hill.

Even with his back to me, the bull is defiant. He's a very different animal than the one I saw with Benny in Colorado. In my new "open" state, I can see power emanating from him. This beast encounters few fences, and it's clear he has enough acreage.

A breeze has picked up, and the cottonwoods in the gullies shiver in the wind. They've all turned a bright yellow that heralds the fall and the coming winter. You can feel the season turning.

It's time for me to move on. As much as TR loved this place, the same thing happened to him.

In 1886, Bill Sewall and Wilmot Dow's wives gave birth to two healthy babies. When they eventually returned to Maine, they called them the Badland Babies. One of their sons was the man who sold us our land.

TR said later in life that the only reason he ever went on to father children again was because he got to watch those two women go through healthy pregnancies while they lived together on the ranch.

All six Mainers left the state before the next winter set in.

During the 'starvation' winter of 1887, TR lost sixty percent of his stock. He quit the ranch after that, only returning a handful of times, but talked about his experiences in the Dakotas for the rest of his life.

And after he arrested Red Finnegan, he was a different man.

Two weeks later, in a bar in Dickinson, some guy called him 'four eyes,' and TR leveled him with a punch. His escapade with Red turned him from a 'dude from New York' into a 'Westerner,' and that man would not be held down—ever again.

The Elkhorn Ranch Site is a protected national park unit, and his former writing desk is on display at the park center.

As I drove away, I felt that the entire place was a shrine to Theodore Roosevelt, and as a fan of our national park system, I was okay with that.

I can sense Edward Abbey trying to speak up from the back of my mind, but I'm feeling stronger today and manage to keep him at bay.

I get on the highway and play some Johnny Cash. I begin with one of my favorites, a best-known song, although his wife, June Carter wrote in, not him.

Cruise control is set to five over the limit. Roman hops on the middle console and defiantly stares ahead. We're on the road again.

Love is a burning thing
And it makes a fiery ring
Bound by wild desire
I fell into a ring of fire

Walt Whitman
(1819 - 1892)

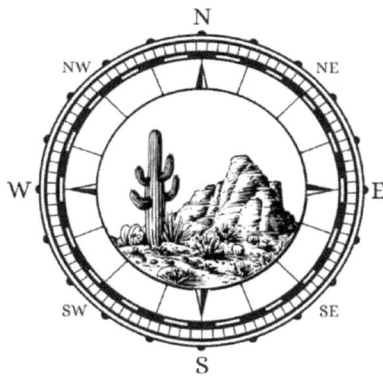

The Missouri River by Sioux City.

Chapter Six

IOWA

We exit the park, and I fill up at the same sketchy gas station in Medora. I feel like that hazy glow that's been blocking out the sun is now around me. Everything is muffled.

I am distant—whitewashed.

I wish I was still surrounded by animals, not people.

I keep getting flashes of waking on the prairie.

When I enter the store, I keep my head down. I don't make eye contact or chat with the two guys who remind me I can save three percent if I pay cash or the man who rings me up.

All the tourist nicknacks grate on my nerves, but I do have the sense to grab a few pricey powerbars so I don't starve to death.

Once we are back on I-94, I begin to relax.

Roman settles down as well. I scoop out a bowl of his food and set it on the seat next to him. He sniffs it but leaves it be for now.

Our next goal is Chanute, Kansas, about a thousand miles away. I doubt like hell I'll make it in a day. Maybe Sioux Falls, which is about two-thirds of the way there, but we'll see. For now, it'll be six or seven hours heading dead east until I can pick up I-29 south.

The horizon melts into the far distance, enveloped in that haze from B.C. fires again. And as we blaze east, the land seems fabricated to me. Created on a production line to achieve that unnatural flatness. If I lived here, I might just become a flat-earther because it seems "Someone" forgot to include a curve in the design.

I feel hypnotized as I cruise down the road. I munch down a powerbar, offering a third to Roman. He happily snatches it.

It seems like we've reached Bismark in no time, but when I glance at the clock, I see we've been on the road for ninety minutes. I've been driving silent, with no radio or Spotify. And it seems my mind has been simply off; I don't think about anything as I plod along, which is a nice change of pace.

The road is straight and unchanging in its expansive bleakness. I'm used to big horizons after living in the Southwest for the last twenty years, but this place is crazy.

We pass over the Missouri River as we cut through Bismark. If we could follow the river directly southeast, it would only be 400 miles to Sioux City, but instead, we're gonna add another hundred miles by driving to Fargo because I need to pick up the interstate.

I drift back to the sunrise I witnessed. I'm still squinting at those first rays of light, diffused and silent in the early morning. A few birds call out plaintively. The endless, undulating land is calm and serene as it prepares for a new day. The tall grasses of the prairie lean and weave in a gentle breeze. There's a rugged grandeur at work here — one that stirs the soul.

Suddenly, a bison emerges on a nearby hill. The sun's gentle light silhouettes his dark, shaggy coat in gold. He's a colossus, an ancient guardian. I am drawn to this magnificent creature that sways in timeless harmony.

The bull walks to my vehicle, his steps slow and deliberate. He pauses only a few feet from my open window. He stares at me. We share a moment — and suddenly, "nature" is no longer something detached. I'm in touch with another consciousness. Something living. And we're communicating!

He could destroy *the Heat* easily if he wanted to; I've seen videos of it on YouTube at this very location. But there's no malice with me here right now—only grandeur and splendor. I'm locked in a timeless moment. His russet coat is redolent with the earthy scent of the plains. I want this moment to go on forever. There are no other cars on the park road at this hour, so more bison spill onto the pavement and plod away from me.

But the bull stands beside me for another ten minutes, not in a rush to leave or follow the herd.

I want to embrace him and leave the safety of my car, but I know better. Yet, I have a strong desire to hold on to this experience, to not let it go.

As I drive down the highway, I can still feel his eyes on me.

As we approach Fargo, I notice the grass has gotten lusher. We're in the tall-grass prairie now, and it receives twenty-four to forty inches of rain a year; triple the water of the prairie I drove through on my way from Utah to North Dakota.

At Fargo, I gas up again. I'm about to tear open the other powerbar when I snap out of it long enough to grab a ham and cheese sandwich, which I share with Roman. We're not eating all that healthily, but at least I've managed to lay off the booze.

We're heading south on I-29, and the afternoon sun is streaming in the passenger window. Roman sleeps in a puddle of it, apparently impervious.

Eventually, my mind drifts to my 'spirit walk' the night before. I do, somehow, feel like I communed with both Benny and my mom. I'm not entirely sure what all that stuff with Theodore Roosevelt was about, but I feel like I connected with him, too.

My goal had been to have a few quiet moments with their spirits, but my internal conflicts, mixed with my personal demons, all added to an overwhelming experience. I know; the weed and alcohol didn't help.

I remember the rain tapping my mother's name on the vegetation around me, *Pat.. pat... pat...* and strangely, when I'd been awakened by the sound of bison grazing and moving closer. I'd lain there for a long time, listening to the herd chomping and ripping at the grass. I'd heard them grunting and the clop of their hooves as they approached.

Yet when I'd sat up, the prairie had been empty for miles.

It had all filled me with wonder: the smell of the earth, the whisper of the rain, countless insects throbbing in unison, elk and coyotes crying out. It was so incredibly beautiful that even in remembering, I tear up.

I was grateful that my spirit walk felt like enough. I got to say goodbye—and I felt heard. I can imagine how taxing it must be to try to keep someone alive in your mind. The Lakota Sioux have a bereavement ritual called the Keeping of the Soul, or *Nagi Gluhapi*. This practice entails mourning for a lost loved one by wearing their clothes and pretending to be them while embodying their spirit. During this time, the participant cannot touch knives or sharp objects. They are not allowed to participate in hunts but are welcome to watch from a nearby hill.

During this practice—which can last up to a year—the mourner must wear black and refrain from singing, dancing or enjoying life but only suffer while remembering the lost one.

How tragic that seems to me—not letting the loved one go but instead holding on. Maybe that's what some people need, but I think my mom—and Benny—would prefer to see me enjoying how the light reflected off the river this morning; to watch me get excited for a new day.

Not mourn an old one.

Suddenly, Whitman pops into my head, and I hear the opening lines for his *Song of the Open Road* in my ear.

> *Afoot and light-hearted I take to the open road,*
> *Healthy, free, the world before me,*
> *The long brown path before me leading*
> *wherever I choose.*

I think of Walt Whitman as I weave through the traffic. I hear his words in my head occasionally, but he doesn't bother me. He's never been an apparition like Ruess or Abbey. Instead, I find him comforting.

Born in West Hills, New York, in 1819, he was influenced by Emerson, Thoreau and Oscar Wilde, but his style is truly unique. He is considered the father of free verse.

Uncle Walt believed in transcendentalism: that we each hold a personal knowledge of God, and no intermediary was needed for spiritual insight. He was also a Realist and celebrated the common man and everyday life. And really, why can't an average person experience God — or nirvana — while doing something he or she loves? When else are you supposed to experience it?

I must be getting tired because when I glance across the highway at the oncoming traffic, I see Pirsig on his motorcycle. He's barreling north, not in a rush. In the quick flash of our passing, he glances at me, and his expression says it all.

"You really should be on a motorcycle right now…"

I think Robert Pirsig and Walt Whitman might have gotten along. In *Zen and the Art of Motorcycle Maintenance*, Pirsig dove deep into the roots of the Greek word *arete*. On the surface, the word means simply quality or excellence, but Pirsig believed there was also an aspect of virtue, of individual distinction. The pursuit of quality, or *arete*, was an attempt at achieving the highest state of personal excellence one can reach.

I'm just a layman, just an old man driving down the road lost in his head, but they both seem to be saying: Do something you love, and put your heart into it, and you will find God. Maybe we call God something else — excellence, quality, or *arete* — it doesn't matter to me.

Whitman instilled these concepts into his works, which is why I love his writing so much. As an atheist, I don't believe in a puppet-master God, but I can accept pantheism, the idea that God is part of everyone and everything.

Here are a few lines from *Leaves of Grass*, which he published in 1885 when he was sixty-six.

I hear and behold God in every object,
yet understand God not in the least,
Nor do I understand who there can be
more wonderful than myself.

I drift along, passing Waterton, and then after about five hours of driving since Fargo, I arrive at Sioux Falls. The sun is just about gone as I look for a place to camp or park, but I'm fading now, tired, and before I know it, I've missed the exits.

I continue in the dark and finally take an exit at Sioux City, where random luck sets me at a campground along the Missouri River.

I'm dead tired and stagger out of the Buick when it's finally parked. I paid for a tent site, although I plan on sleeping in the vehicle.

I break out the stove and heat a can of soup.

Roman watches with glittering eyes.

It's fully night now, and a heaven full of stars shines above. It may be early fall here, but it's much warmer than in North Dakota. I set up a camp chair and put a blanket on it.

Roman heads right for it, but I tell him to hold on. He steps in place anxiously, not liking to be stopped this close to chillin'. In a minute, I have a bowl of soup and spoon; and I'm in the chair with the blanket on my lap. Now, he—carefully—hops up on my lap while I hold the soup aside.

Once settled in, we stay like that for an hour—and it's the best hour of my day. I peer through the darkness at the riparian growth along the river, listening to frogs and crickets.

Soon, I make Roman's night when I let him help clean my soup bowl. I may make fun of him from time to time, but he is a good boy—and I tell him so.

I remember thinking about the four-hundred-mile river journey I might have taken from Bismark to get here. How long would that take? Would my back hold out? If only I had the time—and the body—to do a four-hundred-mile river journey. I've had big adventures in my youth—a few epic river sagas among them—but as I get older, I realize you can't hold on to anything.

What you've done is in the past; you need to be content with the present. At least, that's what they tell me, but my mind is still a whirlwind these days. The North Dakota prairie might have helped me along, but I've still got some shit to figure out.

I look at the stars again, and Whitman saves me by pointing out my insignificance.

Let your soul stand cool and composed before a million universes.

Although Whitman's verse was considered controversial in his day because of its explicit sexual imagery, *Leaves of Grass* is often said to be America's second Declaration of Independence.

He was a religious skeptic; he accepted all churches, yet he believed in none. To Whitman, God was both immanent and transcendent.

His words cut straight to the core as they expose the human spirit. They're honest. They make us see what we've lost as much as what we still hold on to. He wrote *O Captain! My Captain!* in response to the assassination of President Lincoln, and it became his best-known poem in his lifetime.

O Captain! My Captain! Our fearful trip is done,
The ship has weather'd every rack,
The prize we sought is won,

In this case, the ship is the country that has just survived a civil war. In the poem, the Captain has "fallen cold and dead" on the deck, like Lincoln in the war's final months.

He sought to explain the essence of human experience by celebrating everyday life—and the individual.

> *Not I, not anyone else, can travel that road for you.*
> *You must travel it for yourself.*

He preached a doctrine that required the reader to judge for themselves what was right or wrong, to be rebellious, free-thinkers, and free doers.

> *Resist much, obey little.*

I think of those episodes when I shouted at the heavens and wonder who exactly I was addressing. It's happened in the Amazon, the Thar desert, the Annapurnas — all remote places away from civilization.

Even though they just occurred, seemingly spontaneously, I know now there was a period in which I was holding something back. I wonder if it was rage or love I was trying to vent. Most times, it felt like a bit of both.

All I know is that sometimes I need to express myself — to scream at someone. To let the heavens feel my wrath. When this happens, I need to be heard.

I will not be patient. I will not have Faith. I am a wolf, not a sheep. I am a nomad. I hear Whitman again…

> *I too am not a bit tamed,*
> *I too am untranslatable,*
> *I sound my barbaric yawp*
> *over the roofs of the world.*

The following day, I sleep through the sunrise, and it's well up by the time I lift my head. I've got less than three hundred miles to drive today, which seems like a cakewalk.

As soon as Roman sees me stir, he begins spinning in a circle and sneezing. I realize he needs to pee, and I scramble over and let him out. "Don't go far!" I shout.

Soon, we are both in the front with the engine running, but instead of returning to the highway, I park at a dinner by the exit. I leave Roman in the Buick, in the shade with the window cracked, and I go in for breakfast.

I leave him a bowl of dry dog food.

He gives a stare, "Really?"

I'm in a funny mood this morning, and I scan the menu for apple pie. Not listed as a dessert. Figures. One of the things that bothered me about *On the Road* was how the protagonist, Sal Paradise, always seemed to be broke but still frequently ended up in a diner or restaurant eating apple pie.

And then everything turned around for him. Magic-fuckin'-pie.

It always seemed like such a luxury to me. In my youth, I barely got by when I first traveled and starved quite a few times, often for a day or two. And sometimes, I barely ate anything substantial for weeks at a time. Of the ten six-month international trips I completed in my twenties, my mom cried on almost every return because of the skinny mess I'd become. At the time, I didn't care; it was simply worth staying on the road. To keep traveling.

I had plenty of friends who did the same thing.

But I was always jealous about the apple pie.

There have been times I would have done some crazy shit for an apple pie. Not kill anyone, mind you. But maybe cross a swamp or hike ten miles through the mountains.

I grew up about twenty miles from Walden Pond, where Henry David Thoreau completed his two-year experiment of self-reliance and simple living. He got by on very little and wrote some pretty good stuff while there, but his mother did his laundry—and supplied him with freshly-baked apple pies each week.

Over the last few years, I've tried a few times to get myself a slice of apple pie, and I always struck out. I found it on a menu in Cottonwood, but after I ordered it, I discovered they were out.

Today, I order coffee, an omelet and a side of bacon.

Occasionally, I glance up at some of the other occupants.

Everyone knows each other. Baseball caps. Fleece vests.

They're all wondering who the fuck this strange tourist is.

I feel like I'm on Campbell's Hero's Journey again, although, like *Follow Your Bliss*, that journey is greatly misunderstood. It's not only about a hero going on an epic quest and returning triumphant but also about the trials, challenges, and wisdom gained. There doesn't have to be a lofty goal, either; you might just be going to the post office and back. And it's more than an external adventure; the Hero's Journey is an internal one that leads to self-discovery and transformation.

I always returned home a train wreck. Skinny, broke, and very uncertain of what I'd just experienced or what I thought of it.

I finish everything on my plate except two pieces of bacon, which I wrap in a napkin for Roman. Then, I leave a tip on the table and pay the tab at the counter by the door. As I walk to the Buick, I realize that, aside from ordering, I haven't said a word.

But that all changes when I open the door. Roman acts like I've been gone a week and dives for me. "Easy — settle down — easy!"

He smells the bacon before I even sit down and attacks me with his nose. I push him away, unwrap the bacon, and hand him a piece.

He smiles and wags his tail. "That's more like it."

As I get back on the highway, my mind is still spinning over the Hero's Journey. We've got over two hundred miles to Kansas City, and I'm thinking about its dark side.

To learn or experience something "new," the hero must leave his (or her) comfort zone. He must travel somewhere strange or do something very different. He must sacrifice security. Only then can he gain new knowledge.

But upon his return, he often finds people don't want to hear this new truth. They don't like change — they hate it. Especially if it requires them to alter their beliefs, be they political or, heaven forbid, religious.

When I returned from Central America in the 1980s, friends and family argued with me about the US's benevolent intentions in places like Nicaragua and Panama. They said the Contras were helping to preserve Democracy and that they were freedom fighters.

When I told them I'd seen school buses full of children blown up by the Contras, they said I'd misunderstood what had happened. I'd gotten it wrong. It was mind-blowing to encounter people who would trust their news source — often an entertainment channel — over someone who just returned from the place. I'm no hardened journalist — but I know what I saw.

Also, in the nineties, after a trip to the Amazon, I began trying to convince friends of the dangers of Climate Change and the impending loss of life, only to be laughed at for the next ten years because everyone thought I was exaggerating. Even now, thirty years later — with two-thirds of the wildlife on the planet gone — I still have skeptical friends who tell me it's just weather.

So, what is the sense of traveling or growing if you can't share it? Karl Jung had an expression: *gnostic intermediary*. It means someone who expresses what he learns through action, not words. But sometimes, your journey gives you lessons you don't necessarily want to share or teach.

In college, I used to take the bus to Attleboro, Mass., where I would spend a weekend staying with my Aunt Marcia. I'd share a glass of wine with her and watch movies from her couch.

One Friday night, I was restless, and in the middle of the show, I told her I was going to step out and take a walk. She raised an eyebrow but said nothing.

I left her house and walked across Capron Park to a liquor store, where I bought a six-pack of beer. I was only nineteen, but the guy didn't card me.

When I stepped outside, two young women in a blue Nova said hi and began chatting. They were my age, and one was pretty and overly friendly. Before long, I was sitting in the back seat with her while her friend drove us around.

They turned down a side street and then onto a dirt road, where they parked. It looked like the town party spot. The one in the back began to kiss me while the one in the front cracked open one of my beers. I couldn't believe my luck.

After about ten minutes, a pickup pulled up and parked about fifty feet away. Three guys got out, one of them yelling and screaming. As I watched, he slammed his head into the hood of the truck repeatedly. His friends tried to calm him down.

"Oh, fuck," said the girl driving, "that's Jimmy."

The guy was all worked up. He raised his fist at the sky and screamed, "Lenore!!!"

I stared at the girl I'd been kissing. I knew then, without a doubt, her name was Lenore. And it was no coincidence we came here to park. "Who the hell is Jimmy?" I asked.

She sighed. "He's my boyfriend — ex-boyfriend. He told me he was gonna do acid with his creepy friends tonight, so I dumped him."

I leaned forward and asked the other girl, as politely as I could, "Can you please get me out of here?"

She sipped my beer, held my stare for a minute, then slowly pulled us forward. When we passed the truck and the men, I saw Jimmy. He had a red welt on his forehead, and there was a trickle of blood.

He took one look at me in the back with his girl and lost his mind. As we passed, he grabbed the door handle, missed it, and slammed both fists down on the trunk, tumbling to the ground as we drove away. As we skidded down the dirt road, I saw the three guys jump into the truck.

We sped away, took a right turn onto a paved road, and just before the driver turned onto a busier road, I quickly stepped out of the car. In a flash, they were gone, and I stepped back into some bushes.

A few seconds later, the truck with Jimmy and the guys came screeching by. As they drove off, I was surprised to see I was holding the six-pack, which was missing a beer.

About a block away, I could see Capron Park. I crossed it and made my way back to Aunt Marcia's couch. When I sat down, my eyes must have been wild because she took one look at me, shook her head, and said, "You never should have left the couch."

I'm unsure what lesson I learned on that Hero's Journey, but it changed my life. Maybe it is simply the value of thinking before entering a stranger's car. But it's typical of my other journeys — I usually stumbled home in awful shape, not certain what I'd experienced.

And I'll never forget sitting on my Aunt Marcia's couch after my return, but knowing now that those fucked up kids were still racing around the town. At that moment, the world outside had changed for me, but not her. In later years, I reflected on the fact that my aunt had been working as an emergency room nurse then, and I wondered what type of "journeys" her work put her through that I was blind to.

In most cases—again, I'm told—this all eventually leads to personal development and self-discovery. But not always. I've been on journeys that still haunt me. I feel a part of me is still exhausted and broken, stumbling through the Annapurnas in Nepal or the South American Andes, just trying to return to civilization.

Some things you just can't escape. I feel that Bill is out there, somewhere. He's not just a ghost, although he's probably an old man by now. But what kind of lesson should I take from that twisted experience?

It's one of the reasons I'm going to Chanute, Kansas, to see my crazy writer friend, Mark A. Patton. Number 1 nicknamed him Question Mark when she was ten, so I will stick with that for now.

It was Question Mark who first talked me into writing down the story of my time with Bill, or as he came to be known, The Butcher. So, I admit I'm visiting him now with some trepidation. It's a past I don't really want to dig up despite the fact that I can't seem to shake it.

And Question Mark has a method you must work through if you want to see any wisdom. It involves binging on weed and alcohol and spouting out quotes from Bukowski or any number of great writers. The first forty-eight hours can be brutal.

The destination hoovers numinously, but I can't imagine going anywhere else. I need a break—and to face my fears. So, I leave Iowa: the birthplace of John Wayne, Aston Kutcher and Elijah Wood. It treated me well, so I shouldn't bitch. I've got about a hundred miles to go, and the day is young.

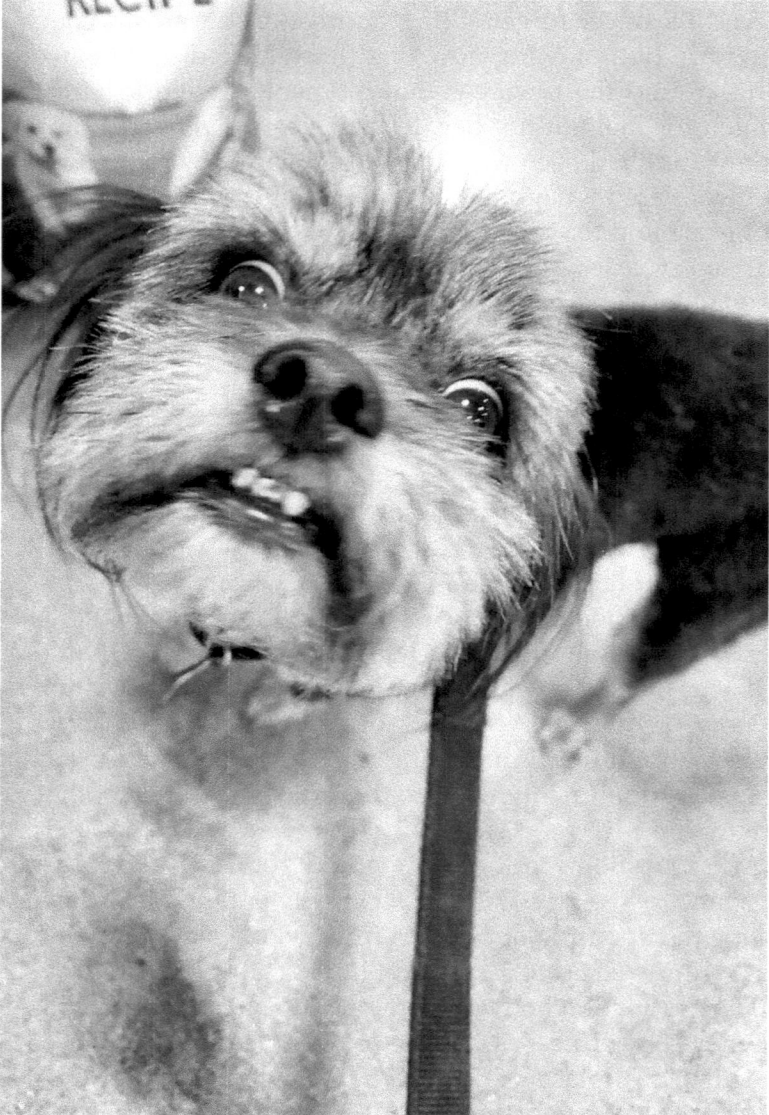

Roman.

Mark Twain, or Samuel Langhorne Clemens
(1835 - 1910)

American Literary Nomads

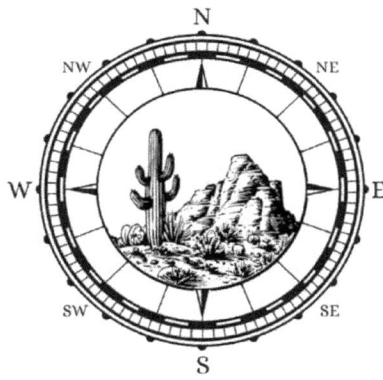

Downtown Chanute, Kansas.

Chapter Seven

KANSAS

I try to skirt to the west of Kansas City as I drive south to Chanute. The traffic isn't bad, and I'm glad I slowed down and had breakfast. When I pass under I-70, I get shivers thinking about Bill.

I suppose because we're going to see Question Mark, and Bill might come up, that I should come clean about him. In 1985, when I was twenty-one, I got picked up by this guy while I was hitchhiking from Los Angeles to New Hampshire.

He seemed like a nice man. He carried a briefcase, was dressed in a business suit, and always talked about appointments. That first morning, at a 7-11 in Flagstaff, he bought me a breakfast burrito. He wasn't going directly east but would be soon, and in the meantime, here he was, buying me breakfast.

I was flat broke, so I went with it.

But I soon discovered he was twisted. By midday, he began to swear and become belligerent. He avoided buildings with cameras. He tore off his button-up shirt, leaving only a sleeveless t-shirt, and suddenly, he was an AWOL soldier called Baker who was gonna kill me if I ratted him out.

He began driving east. I stayed with him, biding my time. This new personality threatened to hunt me down and kill me if I fled because "There was no way he was going back."

And then, at night, when I huddled in the corner of a motel room, he turned into a third person. This one slicked his hair back, had a southern drawl, and was mean. This one saw through my plans to escape. He stole my journal and said if I took off, he'd hunt down my family. He got into my head. He knew I was a writer, and I think he kept me along as an audience.

A witness.

After he stole my journal and read a story about a butcher in Morocco who tried to kill me with a meat cleaver, he had me start calling him The Butcher. The Butcher opened the salesman's briefcase, and I saw it was filled with cocaine. Wherever we went, at night, the Butcher caused chaos, giving away free drugs and messing with people.

And then the next morning, he would wake up, shave, put on a suit, and begin his day as Bill, the salesman—and it would all happen again. I can still see it...

The room's door was unlocked, and I opened it.

To my horror, I saw the Butcher standing there, shaving.

"Morning, pardner," he said with a smile. I was so shocked I couldn't move.

He had on his white shirt and tie, but he no longer looked like a businessman. One eye was swollen and bruised where Jerry had hit him. His knuckles had scabbed over but still looked terrible. He had a disheveled look about him.

In the corner, Jerry lay where he had dropped.

Over the next two weeks, I witnessed things I don't want to talk about. Death threats... blackmail... rape... murder... Sometimes, there were other passengers, but not all of them fared well. I finally escaped in Cortez, Colorado, when me, and another guy from New York, stole Bill's car. We made it to Denver, then got on I-70 heading east. I still feel guilty for just fleeing and not going to the cops, but I was terrified, and he threatened to kill my family.

Even now, when I get on that highway, I seem to lose the ability to breathe.

It doesn't take long for me to reach the outskirts of Chanute. I know Mark lives on the main street, so I'm just following signs and haven't broken out his address yet.

Mark is a screenwriter specializing in horror. Some of his work has made it onto the big screen, but last we talked, he was wrapped up in a few ongoing projects. My favorite, *The Bloody Benders*, is about a family who robbed and killed pioneers passing through this area.

He went to Grinnell and is incredibly well-read. When he lived across the street from me in Sedona, we used to smoke weed, talk about great writers, and then play a little Halo.

He questioned me about my travels back then, having heard a few dozen of my travel stories, and eventually talked me into writing a novel entitled *The Wayward Traveler*. One chapter in it relives my time traveling with the Butcher.

Mark eventually worked with me to convert the chapter featuring the Butcher into a screenplay. At the time, I thought it would be therapeutic to make my baggage into a story; to turn my trauma into drama. It worked fine when I was safe in Sedona, but once I got on the road again, it only made my past with Bill seem more real. I gave him details.

Even now, after all these years, I've just scared myself while I thought about him. I've gotten myself worked up. I glance in the rearview mirror, expecting to see a dark blue Buick Skylark closing in on me.

Then I see myself. My eyes look wild; my hair is a mess.

I pull over on a quiet stretch and try to freshen up. I pop the back hatch and grab a fresh shirt, and while I button it up, Roman pees.

Back in the car, my appearance has improved, but my eyes still look crazy. I try to calm myself by thinking of daughters Number 1, 2 and 3, in that order. I also think of my wife.

She'd be telling me to "Be in the moment—get out of my head."

I take some deep breaths. I start the engine. My plan right now is to go see the only person I know who's madder than me, but let's do it. I can't go home like this, so I'm going to lean into my pain.

I like the looks of Chanute, and I'm glad Mark doesn't live in some busy metropolis. I've read up on the small town and know a little of its history. It was founded in 1873 along the Neosho River. In its day—before everyone moved to the big city—it cast a much bigger shadow. Today, there are about nine thousand residents.

I see signs for a Historical Museum, the Historic Santa Fe Depot, and an Art Gallery. The main street is wide and slow, which suits me fine. About half the storefronts are empty.

These days, I'm not sure why folks visit.

I suppose there's always hunting and fishing.

I see a sign for a Safari Museum and remember Question Mark always talking about it—a strange thing to find in Kansas.

People casually stroll on the sidewalk, and after seeing a few of them, I suddenly realize it's Sunday.

I see his number on the door and park on a side street. A minute later, I'm about to knock when I see him walking my way. The sun is delightful here, and it illuminates him. He's in shape and has lost some weight since I've seen him last—a few years—and there's a lightness about him. For lack of a better word, he seems happy.

Before he gets to me, an old lady passes Mark and greets him.

"Hello!" she exclaims, and after a quick hug, she adds, "God bless you."

Mark smiles broadly, "And God bless you, too."

I almost fall down hearing my staunch atheist friend say those words. This is the guy who raged at a man in the Sedona Walgreens when he told him, "Jesus loves you." This is the guy who first introduced me to Charles Bukowski with the quote…

Find what you love and let it kill you.

Kinda dark if you ask me.

When he sees me, his smile expands, and he envelopes me in a big, hard hug. "Welcome to Chanute," he says. Mark is a big man, a former football player, and his hug is formidable.

"God bless you?" I ask.

He waves it off. "What harm does it do? She's a nice old lady; I've known her all my life. Why not be nice and just go along with it?"

It's a refreshing change, even if I didn't expect it. It makes me want to tone down my atheism. I spent so many years arguing with my dad about religion that it's just second nature to rebel.

I'm still lost in my head when Mark asks, "You hungry? We should eat before we go to my place. My fridge is empty."

My breakfast in Iowa seems like a long time ago, so I clean off the passenger seat and move Roman to the back. It does little good because as soon as Mark is seated, the dog is all over him.

I apologize. "Sorry, he doesn't get many visitors."

Soon, we are seated at a Mexican restaurant. In Sedona, we have a big selection of Mexican restaurants, but only a few of them are decent. Having traveled quite a way from the Southwest, I was hoping for some other type of cuisine, but Mark seems adamant about this place.

They know Mark here, and it seems like only a minute has passed before we've been greeted, our orders taken, and we're set up with chips and salsa.

A cute waitress stops and asks if we want drinks. Mark flirts with her and orders an iced tea. I'm surprised we're not getting margaritas, but I follow suit.

"You're not going to believe the food here," says Mark. "And across the road, there's another Mexican restaurant that's just as good. It's tough to stay in shape with such primo eats just down the street."

I laugh. "Why so much Mexican food in the middle of Kansas?"

Mark munches down a salsa-dipped chip before answering. "In the early to mid-20th century, a lot of Mexican immigrants came to Chanute to work on the Santa Fe Railroad and in the sugar-beet or meatpacking industries. This part of town is known as Little Mexico. Some of the first guys to settle down here actually lived in boxcars that were left over."

Our food arrives, and I take a bite. "It is pretty damn good."

He grins, "I think the Mexican food here is better than it was in Arizona."

It's strange to see my friend so content. If I didn't know better, I'd think there was a woman involved somewhere, but he swears there isn't currently. I was sad when Mark moved away from Sedona, but I find Kansas has worked well for him. I think of Dorothy's final epiphany in *The Wizard of Oz*: "If I ever go looking for my heart's desire again, I'll never look further than my own backyard."

That night, Mark sets me up on the couch in his apartment. It's a nice place, and I'm happy to rest. Roman does a complete search, his sniffer working double-time until he finally settles beside me on the couch.

Mark comes out with two drinks. He hands me one, then sits in a stuffed chair opposite me. On the wall is only one painting, a small, abstract piece done by my youngest daughter, Number 3, who is also Mark's Goddaughter. He calls himself the Anti-Godfather.

He says, "I haven't been drinking, but I'll have one tonight with you."

I nod, "That'll work for me."

I ask, "How's the writing going?"

He grins, "Still trying to keep you white."

I smile, but it irks me a little. A few months ago, Mark showed our screenplay about the Butcher to a producer, and he loved it. It went through several stages of approval, but then we hit a snag with financing.

Apparently, all the money was earmarked for films mainly starring black actors, so they would want the character that played me to be black. I told Mark I didn't care. I didn't mind being a little removed from the film, but he debated with the producer regardless. He pointed out that a black man hitchhiking around Arizona in 1985 would have to worry about a lot more than one psycho with three personalities — half the men who picked him up might have had some prejudice.

Again, I said I didn't care. In my past, I've been saved quite a few times when I'd just about given up. Whether it was the Amazon, Sumatra, or Morocco, the person who saved me was always of color.

I had a similar experience with another of my novels about that young vagabond, Everett Ruess, who scored a ride with me near Tuba City. Everett was an artist who was very sensitive but utterly fearless. The Navajo and Hopi he encountered befriended him. At one point, he traveled with a Navajo medicine man.

I found a producer who loved the screenplay. Again, I made it through quite a few hurdles, and then we heard from financing. At that time, the money was all for Christian movies. They said if I made my story about Everett going into the wilderness and finding Jesus, they could approve it in twenty-four hours — not just Christianity but Jesus himself.

Now, after seeing Mark be sweet to that lady on the sidewalk, I wonder if I should reconsider. But here's the problem with accepting that deal. Everett's father was a minister, and his mother was an artist. He often debated religion with his father. Rather than turn to the gospel for answers, he preferred to find God in the rugged canyons of Utah and Arizona. He believed that when he was alone in the wild, there was a presence he could sense — and it could sense him. He sought out a primal awareness in nature.

My third historical fiction novel, *The King of the Coral Sea,* is about a man named Michael Fomenko who left Australian society in 1958 to live alone in the wild because he felt the same way.

In the end, I passed on the offer. It would have made Everet roll over in his grave.

Mark says,

Almost everyone is born a genius and buried an idiot.

"Here we go," I say, "That's the first Bukowski quote."

He raises his glass. "I'm gonna blame it on the scotch."

I try to think of another Bukowski quote and spy Mark rolling a spliff. I think about Bukowski while he's busy.

Charles Bukowski was a novelist, poet and short story writer. His style was straightforward and unapologetic, often depicting the harsh realities of urban life. Some called him the drunk poet, although he was quite prolific and published over sixty books before he died in 1994.

I give Mark a slight dig. "So, you're not drinking, but you do smoke a little weed?"

Mark nods and fires it up. "That about sums it up."

"So, no more Bukowski?" I ask, "Now that you're mostly sober, you can't still like the drunk poet?"

He laughs. "He's not all that dark, you know. I remember things like *instead of clearing your head – clear your heart,* or *If you have the ability to love, love yourself first."*

I stare at him. "What have you done with my friend? Please tell me!"

He laughs. "I just got tired of hating things."

"You sure there's not a woman somewhere?"

He laughs again, "There are prospects — let's leave it at that."

Then he looks at me and gives me a good stare. He shakes his head. "I guess the more important question is what's going on in your head."

Before I can answer, he holds up his hand.

"We're gonna smoke first, then talk."

Later, we're about as laid-back as Roman on the couch beside me. Mark hands me an ice water and asks, "So, what's up?"

"You're gonna laugh," I say, sobering a bit, "But I still can't shake the feeling that the Butcher is still out there somewhere."

Mark does laugh. "That fuckin' guy? Shit, that was forty years ago—and how old was he then?"

I shrugged. "I don't know… thirty… thirty-five."

"So, he's over seventy now," says Mark, "and my bet is that unstable fuck got himself killed long ago. People like that don't often see old age."

I nod. "It just haunts me a little."

"Look," says Mark, "I could go on about the fifty or sixty real serial killers that roam America—but you'd be better off watching out for bad drivers."

I laugh.

"Seriously," he continues. "There are some horrible drivers out there."

I give him a stare. It's not so easy.

He raises an eyebrow and concentrates. Finally, he looks me in the eye as if still deciding if he should speak. He says, "I remember you saying the Butcher was an AWOL soldier during the day—when he called himself Baker—and that he claimed he'd seen and done ugly things in Central America, particularly Nicaragua."

I nod. "It's part of the reason I eventually volunteered to go down there as a journalist—to write about it. I'd heard bad reports from other sources, of course, but he made me believe America had been an evil force in Central America."

Now Mark is looking at me with a powerful stare as he says, "I won't make you get into it, but over the years, I've heard you talk about various incidents from that six-month journey from Texas to Panama—and not all of them were pleasant."

My tongue seems to have dried out completely, and I'm trying not to think about some of that stuff, but Mark says it for me.

"You were shot at several times, your truck hit more than once, you were around a lot of guns and violence, and you saw many victims — including a school bus that had been filled with children…" he let it all trail while I nod sadly.

He holds up his hands. "Now, I'm not saying that sick fuck deserves any forgiving regardless of how Christian I might suddenly appear, but if you want to understand him better, you might want to think of him as a messed-up Vet."

I took a beat. It had never occurred to me that the angry soldier who ran most of the afternoon might be the most authentic version of Bill Baker. The Butcher certainly wasn't, and it seems the salesman was just a cover. Baker had been angry — but when I saw what was going on through groups like the Contras or Noriega's henchmen, it made me angry, too.

I still felt anger, fear and guilt from my time in Central America.

"That does help me understand him a little better," I say, "and I guess it makes him more of a messed-up human and less of a monster. But I still have a fear that overwhelms me at times."

Mark smiles. "You gotta use that fear. Focus it into something and then put all that stuff behind you — leave it in the dust. I'll give you one last Bukowski quote before I turn off the lights.

Writers are desperate people and when they stop being desperate they stop being writers.

The next day, we go to that museum. I'm a real nerd for 19th-century African exploration, not just Stanely and Livingstone, but Burton and Speke, Barth up north, and Mungo Park in West Africa. My first aspiration was to be Tarzan, and the second was to be one of those men.

The beginning of the 20th century, from 1920-25, was the time of the Great White Hunter. I'm generally not so fond of this era. I know people like Theodore Roosevelt and Carl Akeley killed animals to use as tools to educate the public, and you can argue that doing so saved the mountain gorillas right when they were about to be wiped out, but it still seems like a lot of slaughter.

144

So, I'm a little nervous as we park on North Lincoln Avenue and walk over. I expect a dusty exhibition hall, but instead, I'm quite blown away: clean and nicely painted, organized and doesn't feel crowded because of a well-planned layout. A plaque by the entrance boasts it's the #1 Museum in Kansas.

And there's another surprise. Martin and Osa Johnson were American adventurers, documentary filmmakers, and authors. The Safari Museum that bears their name is dedicated to their legacy. The Johnsons traveled all over Africa and the Pacific between the 1910s and the 1930s. They sent home an incredible, world-class collection of cultural artifacts that are now displayed in stunning exhibits. Here were some people who sought out new places to get to know the people—not kill things or plunder.

They also compiled a vast history of photographs and cinematic works, all at a time when many of these cultures—in places like Borneo—were first encountering modern people. They were pioneers of the ideology of "take only photos, leave only footprints."

We meet the director—a nice guy named Conrad—and after about an hour of strolling around, we leave. It was a nice break from getting up and driving right away.

We meet a mutual friend named Jim at a bar, where he have burgers. I also knew Jim in Sedona, and he's done well since returning to Kansas. He's got a good job and a girlfriend, and he's doing well with his daughter—it's good to see him. The only strange thing is that he's since become a Flat Earther, and that's something I really can't fathom. I sit there being polite, but all I want to do is ask him questions.

He leaves before us, and I ask Mark about it.

"I don't know, Jim's always believed some strange shit," he says, "I just stay away from it."

I marvel at his ability to not let things bother him. I should learn from that.

The next day, I feel better. I got a good night's sleep — two of them, in fact — and Mark has steadily been filling me up with Mexican food. Before I drive off, he walks me to a drug store where I buy a charger for my cell.

"Call your wife," he says, "I know you're trying to give her space, but she chills you out. And give those girls a hug from Question Mark."

I tell him I will, and we hit the road. By the time we reach Kansas City, the morning traffic is tapering off. I don't even think about my issues until I turn onto I-70, and then it all floods back.

It was forty years ago on this very stretch of highway when I was twenty-one and penniless, but it seems like yesterday…

Suddenly, I'm in the Butcher's Skylark again, having stolen it the night before. I'm with a guy named Jerry from New York. He's got a criminal record, but I trust him, and we're both just trying to get home.

We've been driving all night — six hours — since we fled the biker house in Cortez. The Rocky Mountains were cold; the car's heater didn't work, and one window was stuck halfway because the Butcher had tried to break it as we pulled away.

I shiver all night and curse him for taking my sweater.

I explore the Skylark's stash spaces and find five dollars' worth of change, a few candy bars in the glove box, and the remnants of a joint in the ashtray.

I hold it up, but Jerry says, "We need clear heads."

He's been too worked up to let me drive. He's in his mid-thirties, just got out of jail, and will do time if he gets arrested for anything because of the Three Strikes policy, but he doesn't care right now as he flies down the highway doing twenty over the limit.

Like me, all he wants to do is get away from the Butcher.

"I'm not stopping until we get to New York," he says.

I don't think we have enough gas money to make it that far.

Jerry continues to drive, even once he begins to nod off. He's sweating nervously and keeps wiping his hands on his jeans.

Suddenly, we almost crash into the guardrail, but Jerry snaps his head up just in time. "You drive," he says and pulls over. As soon as we're stopped, he jumps out and runs around the front while I slid across to the driver's seat. Within a few seconds, we are rolling again.

Jerry digs the joint out of the ashtray, lights it and sucks on it like it's a life support system. Then he turns around in his seat and stares into the darkness behind us.

He says, "I can't shake the feeling that we're not done with him."

My mind slowly returns to the present. To *the Heat* and my steadfast companion, Roman. I shake off that past and tell myself I won't fear a seventy-five-year-old man who is most likely dead. I keep thinking about the violent episodes I witnessed in Nicaragua and wonder how similar they were to what Baker saw and did. I was no soldier, but we both saw death.

I chuckle when I think of the screenplay that Mark and I wrote. When I completed the rough draft, I ended the story with us getting away and fleeing Cortez, but the movie guys Mark worked with wanted an extended finale. They needed a Hollywood ending.

The one we eventually wrote had the Butcher finding me in Hollis, New Hampshire, after tracking down an address in my journal. He shows up at my parent's house, where he threatens to kill them both and then me.

I loved the twist at the end, where we discover that my dad, Ron, is a hitman. That's the family business I've been running from, and after Ron kills the Butcher in our barn, my dad and I bond as he shows me how to dispose of a body—in the Nashua River, of course.

That's more like it. I decide then and there if the Butcher finds me on the road, I'll kill him in the barn. I know I said I understood him better now, but that doesn't mean he gets to join my flock. Nomads are wolves, after all, not sheep, but I like to think we watch over the sheep when we can.

It might seem a little violent to you, but it relaxes me.

I set the cruise to five over the limit, and Roman jumps up on the middle console—we're on the road again.

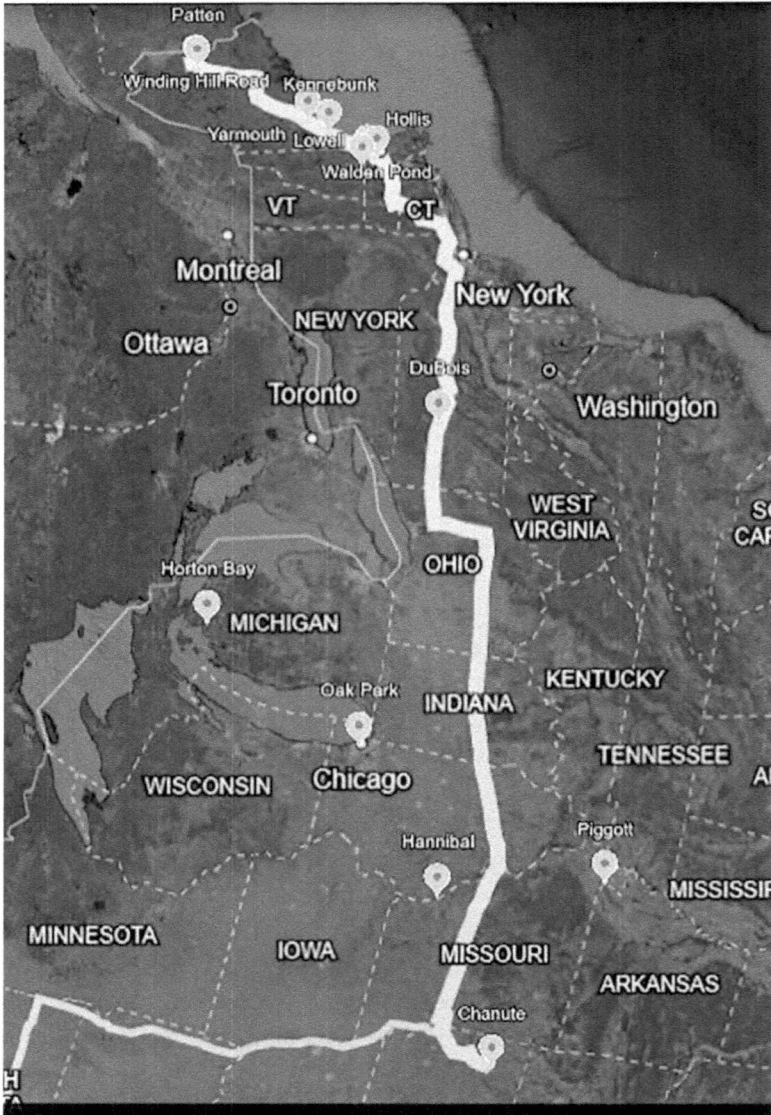

Map 3: Chanute, Kansas to Crystal, Maine.
(1,699 miles.)

Ernest Hemingway at his typewriter.
(1899 - 1961)

American Literary Nomads

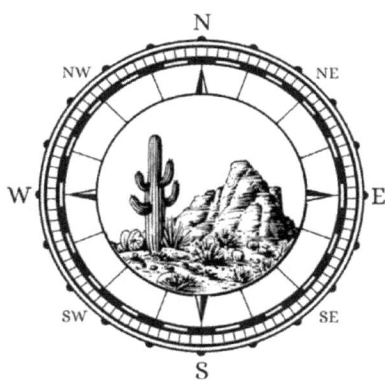

Ohio farm along the highway.

Chapter Eight

OHIO

*G*radually, the plains slip away. I'm so used to the endless vistas of Monument Valley and the North Dakota prairie that I've taken them for granted. Rolling hills now creep in, complete with tufts of woods and small ponds. It seems idyllic. Everything is green, even with fall approaching. The sunlight is soft and comforting.

I find it a bit unsettling. There's no struggle for life here. I've gotten used to the bleakness of the Navajo lands or the rugged Badlands. I can still feel that bison staring at me, although he's fading. I'm leaving the West.

I glance in my rearview mirror. A car back there has been behind me for a while now. It's dark blue and looks a little like the Butcher's Skylark, although it's tough to tell. Paranoid? Most definitely. I flip up the mirror — I'm better off not looking.

I should stop all the overthinking. I've got a full day of driving ahead of me, and despite my desire to stay off big highways, here I am on I-70, charging east for the foreseeable future. My current goal, St. Louis, is still at least three hours away. The Mississippi River runs through the city, and I look forward to crossing it.

The river, of course, reminds me of Twain. Being from the northeast, my first exposure to the Mississippi River was in novels like *The Adventures of Tom Sawyer* or *Huckleberry Finn*.

He's not a voice in my head. In fact, for some reason, when I imagine Mark Twain, I see the actor Woody Haroldson portraying him in an episode of the old series *Cheers*. I'm unsure why, but I suppose it's better than seeing ghosts again.

My back seat has been suspiciously empty.

So, I drive along, Roman asleep in the passenger seat while I think about Mark Twain and the great river we are approaching. Twain was born Samuel Clemens in Florida, Missouri, in 1835, the same year Halley's Comet appeared. He predicted he'd "go out with it" as well, and seventy-five years later, he passed the day after it made its closest approach to Earth.

He had a rollercoaster of a life filled with incredible successes counterbalanced by devastating personal tragedies. He became wealthy beyond any boyhood dreams, only to experience bankruptcy. He toured widely and was recognized as one of the great writers of his day, but lost a wife, an infant son, and two of his three daughters in his lifetime.

Twain earned a great deal of money from his writings and lectures but invested in ventures that lost most of it. He eventually paid all his creditors in full, even though his bankruptcy relieved him of having to do so.

I included him in my Reading List because of his writings on the West and the Mississippi River. Few people make you feel the excitement of the road like Twain. He wrote five travel books in his lifetime: *The Innocents Abroad* (1869), *Roughing It* (1872), *A Tramp Abroad* (1880), *Life on the Mississippi* (1883), and *Following the Equator* (1897).

Roughing It is a semi-autobiographical travel memoir—a fictionalized account—of his time spent in the Nevada Territory. It recounts his "wild west" years, from 1861 to 1867—basically, all of his late twenties.

Much of the tale can be tedious these days, but his enthusiasm is still contagious. The world was fresh, and he was hungry for gold and adventure while working as a reporter, writer and prospector.

Here he is while on the stagecoach ride to Nevada.

It was a superb summer morning, and all the landscape was brilliant with sunshine. There was a freshness and breeziness, too, and an exhilarating sense of emancipation from all sorts of cares and responsibilities, that almost made us feel that the years we had spent in the close, hot city, toiling and slaving, have been wasted and thrown away.

That's it. I can forgive a lot of rambling for thoughts like that.

Before you know it, we've reached St. Louis. A hundred miles upstream lies Hannibal, where much of Twain's adventures are set. I'm within striking distance of the land of boyhood dreams: life on the river, rafts and forts, no rules or responsibilities...

I see the river glittering below me, but I'm sure I'll crash if I don't stop gawking, so I focus on the road. Young Sam Clemens wanted to be a riverboat pilot more than anything; does navigating these chaotic highways qualify me as a modern-day pilot? As much as I like *The Adventures of Huckleberry Finn*, I am drawn more to his early desires to hit the road. To be a pilot on a steamboat chugging up the Missouri or an explorer charting the upper Amazon.

Here are a few lines from *A Boy's Ambition*.

When we presently got under way and went poking down the broad Ohio, I became a new being, and the subject of my own admiration. I was a traveler! A word had never tasted so good in my mouth before. I had an exultant sense of being bound for mysterious lands and distant climes, which I never have felt in so uplifting a degree since.

To be a traveler and not a tourist! That was one of the first distinctions I remember being incredibly proud of. A tourist goes for a set amount of time, whereas a traveler goes until he's had — for better or worse — a feel for the place.

If I'm being honest, I'll admit to preferring the English spelling, with 2 Ls: Traveller. In my youth, I'd use it defiantly, but in this self-publish world, I now feel I have a duty to write a book in either American, British, or Australian English and stick with that style.

See, even I can change.

My secret? When I say the word, I use two LLs.

When I traveled abroad in the eighties, I saw twenty Brits or twenty Australians for every American—and we outnumbered them twenty to one, so it should have been the opposite. During those years, I loved that there weren't many other Americans in Asia or Africa.

The first Mark Twain quote I learned was…

I'm not an American – I'm The American.

I've now got Indianapolis in the crosshairs. I'm flowing along with traffic, letting that reptilian brain take over; creeping out of my default brain. Roman is still sleeping, and although I know I should stop and stretch, I feel like I'm making good time, so I don't.

Suddenly, I'm traveling again—not fleeing my past. It seems everything is in front of me now, not behind me. I don't know how long it'll last, so I will hold on to it. Did just thinking about Twain and boyhood adventures on the Mississippi do that?

North of me is Michigan's upper peninsula. Ernest Hemingway lived in the area with his first wife in Horton Bay, and he often yearned to return to that wilderness. In my milk crate full of books are several by Hemingway. I devoured all his novels and short stories in my teens before traveling, but I haven't read him since.

But I remember the Nick Adams stories and think I might try one out when I stop for the night.

Thanks to Question Mark, I've now got a phone charger, and sooner or later, I'm gonna use it. But for now, I'll ride along in silence and enjoy the feeling of freedom that's hitting me.

I'd like to call daughter Number 1, but she's most likely busy with her baby girl. But she'd get it. She was born a traveler. We conceived her on the Stampede Trail, up in Alaska, and before she turned five, she'd crossed North America five times. When she was sixteen, she had me bring her to get the word *Wanderlust* tattooed on her hip.

I supposed she never had a say in whether she wanted to travel. We just loaded her into the minivan — The Vinniman — with her little sister and hit the road. But then again, none of us do. Some of us wake at night and listen to the Siren's songs as they whisper of distant places. Some of us yearn for the road without knowing it. When I left home at twenty-one to see the world, I'd never met a traveler — someone who had already done it, but I knew I couldn't sit still any longer.

In my case, I became a traveler because I couldn't afford the ticket home. I was hooked the moment I landed in Europe, but within a few short months, I ran out of money. I got lucky and found ways to stay abroad — to stay afloat. I just couldn't seem to make enough to fly home.

In my twenties, I completed ten six-month trips abroad. Almost every time, I ran out of money at some point. Eventually, I got credit cards but never used them until I was confident I'd be in New Hampshire when the bill arrived.

In Africa, I'd start to relax about the time my first sunburn began to peel. The whiteness of my previous life incinerated to help me blend in. Only then did the hustlers on the street back away — a little — because they knew you'd figured out at least a few things by then. You learned to recognize them, even get a grin or a nod when they passed. A place could look so different after a day, or a week, or a month — when you lingered.

Bruce Chatwin captured that raw yearning to immerse yourself in a culture in a story called *Milk*. In the story, a young man sits at a roadside stall in Africa, drinking fresh milk from a gourd. There is a hair in the milk and lumps of cream and froth; as he downs every last drop, he remembers his doctor warning of all the dangers and diseases he'd encountered if he was ever so stupid to travel to Africa.

He could clearly hear the Doctor say, "And whatever you do, don't drink the milk."

In the story, the young man wipes his chin, nods at the vendor, and says, "Another."

Chatwin was an English novelist, travel writer and journalist who blended fact with fiction in stories about nomadic people and exotic places. Even after I became a traveler, I found myself pulled into his writings because of his ability to make you feel more than just a location. I wasn't sure if I'd include him on my List because he's not an American or talking about travel in the US, but he's definitely on this journey with me.

He had a remarkable backstory, too. Chatwin worked once as an art critic and woke up one morning nearly blind. His doctor informed him that he'd damaged his eyes by staring at things too closely and that he should take a leave of absence and focus on horizons. This began a lifelong passion for nomadic cultures.

His first two books, *In Patagonia* (1977) and *The Songlines* (1987), hooked me, but the two collections that made me feel the road were *Anatomy of Restlessness* (1996) and *What am I doing here?* (1990), both published after he died in 1989.

Here's an excerpt from *Anatomy of Restlessness*:

He had been three weeks on the road. The strangeness of Africa had worn off and somehow, in the heat and light, Africa was less unbelievable than home. It was winter in Vermont. He tried to picture it, but the picture kept slipping from focus, leaving only the heat and light.

In India, it was the opposite. The travelers that looked the worst had only been around a month or two. In the eighties and nineties, you could have an entire wardrobe made for twenty dollars, so the travelers in rags only appeared that way because they wanted to look hardened — they could have a new shirt made for $2.

And it confused the Indians, too, who were still emerging from a caste system that didn't quite understand where to classify grungy, smelly tourists who didn't seem to want to go home.

I get through Indianapolis before the 5:00 p.m. traffic. I'm starting to fade and wish I'd stopped at a rest area. I munch down a powerbar and give a chunk to Roman. I know of a campground near the highway on the other side of Columbus, but I'm not sure if I'll make it that far—the place is about two hundred miles away.

I'm starting to see a lot of signs for revivals and other church affairs and realize I'm entering the Bible Belt. It seems every other building is a church. I wish Twain were here with me now. Now, there's a guy I think I could travel with. I believe I was destined to like him anyway: As an aspiring Atheist, there's no way I couldn't approve of someone who said,

Faith is believing what you know ain't so.

There's something of Whitman in there, too, and I hear him again, both men always encouraging others to question everything.

Resist much, obey little.

I also like Twain because he was balanced. I might not believe in an old-school God who takes sides, but I understand nirvana— or the Godhead if you're a Christian—and how experiencing it can make one feel connected to the world—and yourself.

It's all spiritual enlightenment.

So, I don't necessarily want to throw out everything.

Throughout his life, Twain attended services and engaged in religious discussions, but his most controversial opinions on religion weren't published until after his death. In *Three Statements of the Eighties*, he claimed he believed in an almighty God, but not in any messages, revelations, Providence, holy scriptures such as the Bible, or retribution in the afterlife.

His theology grew more cynical while he wrestled with humanity and the deaths of loved ones, leading to the statement he is now known for:

If Christ were here now there is one thing
he would not be – a Christian.

And that's where he crosses into my anger — one of the root causes of all my issues. I'm disgusted with mankind, or most of us, for our inability to change and become kinder, more sustainable, and more humane. I might, unjustly, pick on religions — but hey, they're the people who are claiming to be in it for the good of mankind. They're the people I expect to show compassion.

The one thing we know about Climate Change is that it will cause a flood of refugees, and this current US population does not seem ready to accept that challenge — even if the refugees are from US soil. So instead, I fear we will stumble around and argue, be greedy pricks, hide behind money and religion and not do anything until we're neck deep.

It's like Churchill said,

You can always count on the Americans to do the right thing,
Once they've exhausted all other possibilities.

I reach the campground just after dark. I was here once before, a few years ago, with daughter Number 3, when we drove across the country. I see her sitting on the picnic table as she shyly asks, "Can I get a milkshake with my dinner?"

She would eventually get the shake, and then we watched an episode of *New Girl* in the tent on my tablet.

The tent sites have parking spots, so I'll just sleep in the back of the Buick tonight. They have a nice little restaurant where I order a chicken sandwich with fries. No shake this time.

By the time I crawl into the back, I'm plum exhausted. I lost an hour somewhere, and it's later than I thought. I figure I've driven about six hundred and fifty miles.

I give Roman a few fries that I set aside, and then we snuggle up in the back.

"I gave you my son's room," said the old man, "because you remind me of him—it was not an easy thing for me because your country paid for his murderers."

I woke to these words, spoken to me by a man named Manuel in Nicaragua in the 80s. Two of his sons had been taken by the Contras and executed, and we both knew the US funded the mercenaries. He would become my friend, although I never got used to the sad look in his eyes.

It took me a while to realize where I was… what journey… what state… the campground. I felt Roman beside me and caressed his side. It didn't surprise me that I'd dreamt about Nicaragua; this whirlwind of a road trip seems to be uniting all sorts of events from my past. I lay there for a while thinking about Bill Baker.

In 1988, I volunteered to drive the length of Central America to write travel articles. I did this in part because of the Butcher and my time with him. During the day, he called himself Baker and said he was an AWOL soldier and ranted about the US involvement in places like Nicaragua and Panama. I'd heard concerning reports, too, from European friends, although they differed from the patriotic pitch Reagan and then Bush used to describe the events on the US news channels.

The sobering truth was that my country, regardless of good intentions, was responsible for most of the destruction I saw in Central America. The trip soured me on American politics, and I never wrote about it again, switching instead to exploration, the environment, or historical fiction.

My journey ended violently, too, with me getting beaten unconscious in Panama by a mob when I was delirious with hepatitis, and for years, I had nightmares.

Today, I try to shrug it off. The sun is up an hour earlier than I'm used to, but I'm not in a rush to fight the commuters. I pick up the Hemingway collection and start reading.

Later, I've freshened up—so has Roman—and we're loaded up in the Buick with two bacon and egg sandwiches. I gas up and grab a coffee before hopping onto Route 71. I'll follow it northeast, onto 76 and then 80 as we make the long crossing of Pennsylvania.

I break one of the sandwiches in half and share it with Roman, who gives me his best smile.

We listen to a little Johhny Cash, and I drift back to Hemingway and the story I read. Ernest was born in 1899 in Oak Park, Illinois, and spent his early years there. We probably passed it while crossing Missouri, but there's not much to see there concerning him today.

Later, he lived in Key West, Florida, with his second wife, Pauline Pfeiffer. At St. Louis, I could have jetted south to Piggott, Arkansas, the site of the Hemingway-Pfeiffer Museum, but I've slipped out of "tourist" mode—I've now got momentum.

He began his writing career as a journalist, but before his death at the age of sixty-two, he wrote seven novels and six collections of short stories. His distinctive style, known for its directness and economy of language, is often compared to that of a reporter, where the priority is to be clear, concise and factual.

And there was often much more going on than meets the eye. Hemingway believed in the "iceberg" theory when it came to writing; that the reader sees only the tip of what's there.

Big Two-Hearted River is a short story set in Michigan's Upper Peninsula. The story follows Nick Adams as he hops off a train and finds himself standing next to a burnt-out town. The year before, a fire had ravaged the area. Everything was blackened: buildings, shacks, even signposts, and all the surrounding woods.

He follows a stream, cutting through the charred hills, until he comes to an untouched section of forest near the junction of where the stream flows into a swamp.

Nick is fresh from a traumatic experience, or at least Earnest Hemingway is, having served as an ambulance driver with the American Red Cross while he was stationed in Italy during WWI. He describes the blackened husks of the ancient trees without emotion as he searches the countryside for a campsite — and a place to fish — but just being there seems to relieve him of a burden.

His muscles ached and the day was hot, but Nick felt happy. He felt he had left everything behind, the need for thinking, the need to write, other needs. It was all back of him.

Hemingway had been hit by Austrian mortar fire and sustained significant shrapnel wounds to both legs, but his character, Nick, mentions none of that. His wounds are emotional, and he is seeking solace in nature.

Even so, in some ways, he barely sees the burnt land he traverses until he finally gets a line in the water. The story gave me flashbacks of when I first arrived in Managua, the capital of Nicaragua, in the eighties. I thought it was a futuristic city because of all the green spaces they'd allowed between buildings, but soon, I learned that there had been buildings that'd just been blown up. With up to seventy inches of rain a year and being in the tropics and only 11 degrees north of the equator, grass and trees moved in right away.

Today, when I see plans for anything, say a new development, in all the empty spaces, I see where ghost buildings were.

We pass by Akron, and it takes an hour or so to reach the border of Pennsylvania after that. I'll be on the Pennsylvania Turnpike for about three hundred and fifty miles, and before I'm done, I'll be less than five hundred miles from New Hampshire.

The highway is tight and curvy, like a racetrack. I remember when I drove through with Number 3, a big black bear ran in front of us on one lonely stretch.

I hold the wheel at 10 and 2 while I think about the Hemingway story again. I imagine Nick Adams wandering the charred land in much the same way that I drifted through Managua — not seeing the destruction before him. In his case, it was because he was trying to see the past.

For me, there's something incredibly luring about going to a place that looks destroyed and then finding a little bit of paradise still there. A little bit of the way it used to be.

Nick gets that feeling when he hooks his first fish.

There was a tug on the line. Nick pulled against the taut line. It was his first strike. Holding the now living rod across the current, he brought in the line with his left hand. The rod bent in jerks, the trout pumping against the current. Nick knew it was a small one. He lifted the rod straight up in the air. It bowed with the pull.

And in that moment of visitation, to feel all the old things — all the old feelings — that's what we all yearn for. That's why I included this book in my Reading List. I know the truth is the story is a composite of several trips on a few different rivers, and much of it was with companions. But I like how he wrote it. It makes me wish I knew how to fly fish.

On his second day, he hooks the big one, although he's destined to lose it. You might be able to glimpse the past, but you'll never outshine it.

His mouth dry, his heart down, Nick reeled in. He had never seen so big a trout. There was a heaviness, a power not to be held, and then the bulk of him, as he jumped. He looked as broad as a salmon.

It's the world that used to be. Think of any place your father or your grandfather used to go, and you can bet your bottom dollar it's not as nice as it was in their day. We've squandered our resources like selfish children, with no thought to what's sustainable. Now, with the world's environments in flux, will we embrace the situation and own up to the fact that it's a mess of our own making?

On his final day, Nick looks at the junction of where the river flows into the swamp but decides he isn't ready to fish it yet.

Is the swamp "facing reality" or "facing his past"? We don't know. As a writer, I'd guess creating *Big Two-Hearted River* was his way of exploring the swamp.

Nick did not want to go in there now. He felt a reaction against deep wading with the water deepening up under his armpits to hook big trout in places impossible to land them…. …In the swamp fishing was a tragic adventure. Nick did not want it. He did not want to go down the stream any farther today.

I've gone only a hundred miles or so when a wave of tiredness hits me. I'm approaching the Eastern Continental Divide, and places are becoming more familiar—I'm nearing home—and I've come across another place where I camped with Number 3 on our road trip.

It makes me sad to revisit these places that are so full of memories, but I can't resist. When I pass Dubois, without much thought, I take the exit to the campground.

I stop at the gas station by the exit, knowing this is the only place around, and fill up before entering. Inside, I stare at an empty pie case for a minute before grabbing a hot dogs. I look at the bottles of liquor behind the register, but I've been off the booze for a while, and I think I'll stick with it.

It's only mid-afternoon, and the campground is empty.

I set up my tent while Roman observes. There are little red squirrels here, and when he sees one, he temporarily loses his mind.

So, he's on a leash for now.

After taking a shower, I set up the stove, and soon, the dogs are sizzling. On the other burner, I have a can of beans cooking. Roman knows what's coming and gives me his best smile.

The sunset is just beginning when we crawl into the tent. It's comfortable, especially with Roman, but nothing compared to snuggling with an eleven-year-old after smores. Her presence is so strong I feel like I can smell her. I see her grinning in the dark as she says our catchphrase, "Shrek and Donkey," and I reply, "On the road again."

I know next week she begins testing for her brown belt—one of the reasons she couldn't come this time—and I should call. I've been on the road for a week now and need to snap out of the funk I left in.

My cell charged during the day, and I turn it on now.

There's a whole stack of messages, missed calls, and text messages. I select the one from Number 2.

"Fed the fish. Watered the plants. And turned off the heater by your bed that you forgot. Opened your mail, too. Nothing important. Mom got worried after a few days, but I told her you needed to go walkabout. I figure you're on your way to the cabin, although you didn't seem to know that when we talked last. Ha. I know you better than you do."

That's Number 2 for you. My healer. My sunrise girl. Even as a child, she knew how to relax me. I choke up a little, reading her note, which soothes me. I want to read a few more messages or maybe make a call, but a wave of tiredness hits me, and I drop off into a twelve-hour sleep.

Henry David Thoreau
(1817 – 1862)

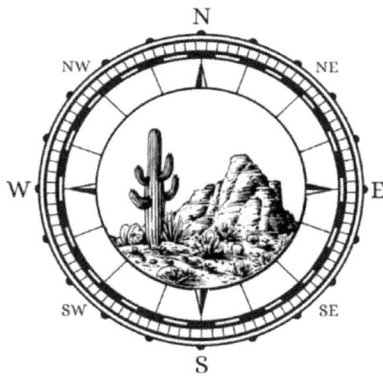

The Mass turnpike.

Chapter Nine

MASSACHUSETTS

I wake with the sun glinting into my tent, reminding me I'm in the mountains on a continental divide. It shines straight from the horizon with what seems a powerful new intensity. For some reason, I feel like it's smiling. I'm in a good mood, and I can't explain it. I feel like I'm floating. Furthermore, it's like I forgot something bad that I'm still supposed to lug around—but for my life, I can't recall what it was.

I nudge Roman, who stares up at me through his overgrown bangs. He needs a haircut.

I ask him, "Who wants to share a power bar for breakfast?"

He butts me with his head, then rubs against me. "You fuckin' know who."

I rip open the package, break off a big piece and give it to him.

Now Roman has the same gleeful look in his eyes as me, as if someone slipped some psilocybin into our blueberry crisp breakfast bar.

I think I'll skip any other nourishment this morning and ignore my appetite for a while even though I have a big day ahead of me— a little hunger makes you think clearer.

I pack up our gear and flip the tent upside down so the dew can dry. While I wait, I do some stretches—my body has a mini-panic attack as I attempt a downward-facing dog pose. All I've been doing is driving or sleeping like a rock; it's like I've been in a trance. I need to move my body. I imagine walking through the quiet woods around the cabin. Stretching my legs as my feet kick through the dew-laden grass on a brisk Maine morning.

There's a youthfulness about our land there; it doesn't feel ancient like the southwest, or maybe that's just my take. As a boy, I always envisioned young Theodore Roosevelt traipsing through the woods. And this wasn't the tormented TR I saw in North Dakota, but a young guy enchanted by the tranquil virgin pine forests and the rugged men who worked there.

I miss that guy and his positive outlook.

I take a quick shower at the campground, my first in a few days.

Before we set out, I try to chase Roman around in the grass, but I'm dizzy and exhausted after two minutes.

Hey, at least I tried.

The Pennsylvania Turnpike is still fast with morning commuters when we first launch onto it, but soon, the traffic tapers off. I'm heading east, and thankfully, because of my casual start, the sun is over the visor. I drift along, trying not to think about anything, and after about a half-hour of successfully doing that, I realize my focus is shifting. I'm no longer looking over my shoulder for Bill's Skylark or hearing Westerners like Abbey or Ruess whispering in my ear. I've also managed to ditch Twain and Hemingway, although they were never a nuisance.

And I haven't started looking east yet. I'm in that limbo stage—traveling—focusing mainly on the car ahead of me or how low the fuel gauge is. I can't believe how lush Pennsylvania is, even with Fall nipping its arrival in splashes of yellow. It seems unfathomable that I was on the Navajo reservation less than a week ago. I pass a horse-drawn buggy with two Quakers sitting up front—and suddenly, this place seems as alien to me as the Indian lands did.

As the miles tick away, my focus slowly, inevitably, slides east—ahead of me. I go over my intended route through New York and then into Connecticut—and from there, I'm only a few hours from New Hampshire—I'm almost home. Well, my old home. Huh.

And just like that, I'm in my head again with a new stack of anxieties. I've got new fears to face—home. Between being born in Massachusetts, raised in New Hampshire, and spending a lot of time at the cabin in Maine, I'm a New England boy, whether I like it or not. I spent half my life trying to get away—especially in the winter—and although I've found a new home in the West, my roots are in the Northeast.

Now, perhaps for the last time, I'm returning.

It won't be the same: my parents are gone, their home sold; my sister is out of town; and brother Dave is pretty busy with work these days, more so now that he's eyeballing retirement. Still, I thought I'd stop in for a night on the way to the cabin.

I make my first call of the trip to my brother and end up leaving a message that I'm passing through on the way to the cabin and could use a bed for the night.

The thought of staying in southern New Hampshire but not at my parents' farm on the Nashua River is difficult to process. Throughout my younger years, when I traveled, Hollis was the safe place that I imagined when I was sick, tired, or terrified. It was the Shire to me, and like most people, my parents seemed like rocks that would never crumble or fade.

I wanted to travel more than anything, but part of what allowed that was having such a solid base. Even if I fought with my dad about travel, at least I had a dad. And no matter how broke or skinny I was, I would eventually stumble home—and it was nice to have a home.

Yet, when I was home, I just wanted to get away. It obsessed me—at times, it was all I thought or talked about. Are there others who have such a restlessness that pursues them so doggedly?

In my bedroom, I secretly scribbled quotes about travel on the wall behind a mirror. The first was from Christopher Columbus's journal, the night before he stumbled upon America (Hispaniola).

They'd seen a few birds, so they knew that land was close.

All night I lay in bed listening to the birds...

As a young man, I couldn't imagine anything better than being an explorer on the verge of a significant discovery. I'm not a big fan of Columbus or just about anything he did, but you get the point.

Most of the other quotes were about the urge to hit the road, like the few from James Taylor songs that made my wall.

Dark and silent late last night,
I think I might have heard the highway calling.
Geese in flight and dogs that bite.
And signs that might be omens say I'm going, going,
I'm gone to Carolina in my mind.

Even small lines seemed to speak to me through the ether, telling me to just start moving—walking, even if it led to limping.

I guess my feet know
Where they want me to go
Walking on a country road.

When I left Hollis, N.H. for Springfield, Mass., to go to college, I tried to put my dreams of travel behind me and follow the path my dad had set forth, beginning with a degree in biomedical engineering so I could install CT, X-ray, and MRI units for his company. I followed obediently despite feeling adrift.

I do not recall dreaming or having dreams in those days. There were no spiritual insights in my studies or yearning for deeper knowledge. Everything was straightforward—just not in the direction I yearned for.

Instead, I sought out "truths" in the lyrics of modern bands.

One of my first bands was Aerosmith. When their debut album came out in 1973, I was only nine years old and didn't quite know what to think of them, but by the time they released *Toys in the Attic* in 1975, I was already scribbling down quotes. They played a dozen shows at the Springfield Civic Center in the 80s, and I believe I caught every one of them.

I remember trying to decipher the lyrics to *Adam's Apple*.

Even Eve in Eden
Voices tried deceivin'
With lies to show the lady the way
At first she stopped and turned
And tried to walk away
Man, he was believer
Lady was deceiver
So the story goes, but you see
The snake was he and she
just climbed right up his tree

Unfortunately, Aerosmith's songs seemed just as confusing as the religious dogma I sought to escape. But they were artists—rockstars—and I felt their drive to express. *Dream On*, which Steven Tyler wrote when he was eighteen, made me feel like a clock was ticking. If I didn't chase my dreams soon, they might fade away…

Half my life's in books' written pages
Lived and learned from fools and from sages
You know it's true
All the things come back to you.
Sing with me, sing for the year
Sing for the laughter and sing for the tear
Sing with me, if it's just for today
Maybe tomorrow the good Lord will take you away

I'm still trying to hold onto that glow I woke up with when Roman and I entered New York. I've been driving for almost four hours, and my back is aching. The word *Equanimity* flashes through my mind, and I chuckle.

A few years ago, I made a big push to get in shape. I began walking every morning and taking weekly stretching and yoga classes. My body didn't like it too much, especially my old lumbar fusion, but I kept pushing through. I dropped twenty pounds, and suddenly, my health issues began fading away.

What got me through was the word *equanimity*.

I've practiced meditation and mindfulness since my twenties, but I learned that equanimity is an entirely different thing. Equanimity refers to the mental attitude of being at peace with the push and pull of experience. Basically, it means accepting discomfort while being aware of it — not letting pain alarm you, just letting it pass through you.

It helped me. A lot. But then I pinched a disc in my back, and it was a long recovery. When I was better, I was too afraid of re-injuring myself, and I stopped taking classes. Now, as I twist uncomfortably, I wonder if I'm not too old to try again.

I find a radio station that's belting out Lou Reed and the Velvet Underground, and I turn up *Sweet Jane*.

There's a sense of resignation to the song as if Jack and Jane only get by because of a little puff they have at night — and I get that — but that buzz also lets them see how "sweet" life is, despite the "evil mothers" who try to convince you that innocence is rare and life is ultimately futile.

> *And there's even some evil mothers*
> *Well, they're gonna tell you that everything is just dirt*
> *You know, that women never really faint*
> *And that villains always blink their eyes, ooh*
> *And that, ya know, children are the only ones who blush*
> *And that life is just to die*

I grab my vape pen, take a hit, and then let out a smokey howl. Roman joins me, and we're singing together just as the chorus hits.

> *Sweet Jane, oh woah*
> *Sweet Jane*
> *Sweet Jane*

We're not in New York long, and by early afternoon, I'm passing Hartford, Connecticut, on my way to Springfield, Mass. I stop at a rest area, let Roman pee, and then run around on the leash because he's a bit out of control after all the pent-up time in *the Heat*.

Then, I fill up the gas tank and use the bathroom.

When I get back in the Buick, I see I missed a call from my brother. He's overnight in northern Vermont on an installation and won't be home tonight—but if I'll be at the cabin this weekend, he'll drive up and see me.

"Good and bad news," I say to Roman. I'd been looking forward to seeing my brother—he always was good at getting me out of my head—but something tells me that I need to get to the cabin first anyway. I'm feeling a profound exhaustion and need a good, long rest and a few solid meals.

I figure it's still almost six hours to the cabin, and I'm unsure if I have that in me. There are not many other options, I suppose. I get on the turnpike and start driving west—we're gonna wing it.

James Taylor plays in my mind, making me wish we were a little later into the fall season.

> *Now the first of December was covered with snow*
> *So was the turnpike from Stockbridge to Boston*
> *Through the Berkshires seemed dreamlike on account of that frosting*
> *With ten miles behind me and ten thousand more to go*

The next verse made it onto my wall of quotes.

> *There's a song that they sing when they take to the highway*
> *A song that they sing when they take to the sea*
> *A song that they sing of their home in the sky*
> *Maybe you can believe it if it helps you to sleep*
> *But singing works just fine for me*

It seems like most of my inspiration in New England came from musicians, not writers. To be honest, most of the writers made me angry. Take Robert Frost, one of the most beloved of our New

Hampshire poets. If I'm going to find a culprit for my wrath, I'll blame him. His poem, *The Road Not Taken* (1915), for some reason, put me over the edge and even made me mad.

This began before I ever hit the road but persisted long after I became a traveler. You're probably laughing at me, but I can't tell you how many times the final lines have come back to haunt me.

> *Two roads diverged in a wood, and I —*
> *I took the one less traveled by,*
> *And that has made all the difference.*

Most people who quote the poem around me usually get it backward and call it *The Road Less Traveled* (It's *The Road Not Taken*). Frost claimed he took the road less traveled, and that "made all the difference," yet the poem is about a yearning for the road not taken. I'm not sure what Frost was saying. Did he wish he'd lived an ordinary life, not one of a poet or artist? Or maybe he just ignored his own title.

He did live a simple life, spending most of it teaching while living on farms in New Hampshire and Vermont. When I was younger, I didn't feel that writing poetry or teaching was unorthodox, certainly not meriting the title "a road less traveled." I would agree that they are necessary and deserve praise, but they are not rare.

When I traveled, I seldom sensed I was on a road that hadn't been traveled before me for millennia. Anywhere I went in Asia in the 80s was filled with stories of all the hippies from the 60s, and I'm sure those hippies got an earful about the people who came before them. You're not going to find a 'road less traveled' in the physical world — especially now — with cell phones.

I guess it just trips me up how many people so casually throw out "road less traveled." Being an artist is a road less traveled; I've heard less than 5% of the population are artists, and that's most likely a good thing. It's not easy having something inside you that you'll sacrifice almost anything to get out — if you are lucky enough to have a way to express yourself.

The individual search for God is a road less traveled. Sorry, but in my eyes, if you are looking within a religion, you're not looking. My favorite book, *The Razor's Edge* by Summerset Maugham, follows a man named Larry Darrell who searches for a deeper meaning to life—spiritual enlightenment. It's a wonderful book, and I am sure it has inspired others to look a little further into what they hold important.

I do feel I should have given Frost a break. It was just one poem, and it was my issues that tripped me up, not his poetry. I dug into other poems, like *Nothing Gold Can Stay*, and found that I could still enjoy his poetry if I chilled myself out.

> *Nature's first green is gold, Her hardest hue to hold.*
> *Her early leaf's a flower; But only so an hour.*

And from *Stopping by Woods on a Snowy Evening*…

> *The woods are lovely, dark and deep,*
> *But I have promises to keep,*
> *And miles to go before I sleep.*

Then I read these lines about walking alone in the night and felt his loneliness and isolation. I remember so many nights when I'd been in similar situations. Suddenly, he was a kindred spirit.

> *I have been one acquainted with the night.*
> *I have walked out in rain — and back in rain.*
> *I have outwalked the furthest city light.*
> *I have looked down the saddest city lane.*
> *I have passed by the watchman on his beat*
> *And dropped my eyes, unwilling to explain.*

Frost might not have lived a road less traveled, but many of his observations ring true—I decide to give him a break. After about an hour, we reach 495, and I get on it, heading north as it wraps around Boston.

I see signs for Concord and think of Walden Pond.

When I was young, Henry David Thoreau seemed like THE anti-traveler. He appeared to go out of his way to despise travel, and because I grew up not many miles from Walden Pond, I heard a lot about him in school.

Me-thinks, I should be content to sit at the backdoor in Concord, under the poplar tree, henceforth forever.

In my twenties, that kind of contentment, for some reason, made me want to choke someone. I yearned so badly to travel and couldn't believe someone could be so content that they could just remain sitting somewhere "forever."

Paul Theroux wrote about what other writers were doing at the time that Thoreau was living on Walden Pond in his incredible collection of essays, *Figures in a Landscape: People and Places.* "Emerson and Hawthorne went to England, Washington Irving to Spain, and Melville to the Pacific. The other travelers of his day: Sir Richard Burton in Arabia and Africa, Sir John Franklin in the Arctic, Sir Joseph Hooker in Tibet, Henry Walter Bates on the Amazon, Darwin in the Galapagos, Alfred Russel Wallace in the Far East. While Thoreau was hiking and paddling in the Maine woods, John Fremont and Kit Carson were exploring the Rocky Mountains. Thoreau read about them all but was not impressed."

It drove me crazy. The only time he mentioned foreign places was to demean them. He claimed he'd experienced a more profound wilderness in northern Maine than most of these men had, whether in the Arctic or the remote Pacific.

It is not worth the while to go around the world to count the cats in Zanzibar.

That quote always makes me smile because it reminds me of my own experience in Zanzibar. Once, while staying in the oldest part of Zanzibar, Stone Town, I became incredibly sick with food poisoning. I lay on my bathroom floor, which was plastered, lime-washed, and hundreds of years old.

For hours, I writhed in pain, at times wondering if I would die there. About an hour before sunrise, I began to surface. I sat up, cleaned up the best I could, and dragged my sweat-soaked body to the roof, where a gentle breeze blew off the Indian Ocean.

At first, I couldn't see much, but as the horizon lightened, I made out ravens in the trees and storks standing down by the water. And there were cats! Scrawny, wharf cats that scurried about in the gloom, sometimes right beneath the feet of the motionless storks, and I wondered if any of them ever got pecked. I'd come so close to death in the night — at least that's how I felt — and I was overcome with gratitude that I was there, watching the sunrise — and counting cats.

Put that in your pipe, Mr. Thoreau.

And then there's the apple pies. Thoreau spent most of his life at his family home. I think I mentioned earlier that when he lived at Walden Pond, his mother still did his laundry every week — and supplied him with pies.

Free Apple fuckin' pies — delivered! I bet it solved all his problems.

My stomach growls at the thought of it. I know I planned a little fast today, but I'm beginning to fade.

However, my opinion of Thoreau changed during this trip. *Walden* is in my crate of books, and every now and then, I flip through it and read phrases I highlighted. It amazes me how the book has an entirely different tone to me now. I no longer notice the slights of foreign places, but instead am drawn to passages that I can't believe didn't jump out to me when I was younger, like this one about pursuing your dreams.

I learned this, at least, by my experiment: that if one advances confidently in the direction of his dreams, and endeavors to live the life which he has imagined, he will meet with a success unexpected in common hours.

I was alone for most of my twenties. For each of my ten big trips, I left alone and returned home alone six months later. I felt isolated at times but also peaceful, especially when in the wilderness. Last night, this quote jumped out at me, making me appreciate the seclusion of my current journey and value Roman as a good traveling companion.

> *I find it wholesome to be alone the greater part of the time.*
> *To be in company, even with the best, is soon wearisome and dissipating.*
> *I love to be alone. I never found the companion that was so*
> *companionable as solitude.*

Thoreau didn't hate other places as much as I thought—he just loved where he was, especially if he was in nature. He loved being a "local" and prized even more traveling in America.

He set the attitude on how to show you care about the country, what tone to use, and what subjects to address, and in doing so, became our first environmentalist. He's been described as "one of the most sensitive and scrupulous noticers of nature and man," and as an older adult, I see why now.

> *We need the tonic of wildness… At the same time that we are earnest to*
> *explore and learn all things, we require that all things be mysterious and*
> *unexplorable, that land and sea be indefinitely wild, unsurveyed*
> *and unfathomed by us because unfathomable.*
> *We can never have enough of nature.*

Thoreau had a unique perspective, guided by strong views on integrity and morality. He wanted his readers to develop their own perspectives and not cave into common thoughts. He believed in the pursuit of spiritual development.

Walden explored the virtues of simple living and self-sufficiency. It is a blend of memoir, sermon and manifesto; through it, Thoreau explains how to live a meaningful life.

> *I went to the woods because I wished to live deliberately,*
> *to front only the essential facts of life, and see if I could not learn*
> *what it had to teach, and not, when I came to die,*
> *discover that I had not lived.*

The traffic is more aggressive here, and over the course of the day, I try to keep up—but it seems to be increasingly busier. Everyone is in a rush. We pass Lowell, and I trip back to Jack Kerouac, who was born there in 1922. He died in 1969 at the age of fifty-seven from abdominal bleeding caused by a lifetime of heavy drinking.

He had several other books, but none as popular as *On the Road*, which he wrote in a three-week, Benzedrine-fueled frenzy on a 120-foot scroll without a single paragraph break. I found reading it exhausting. When Truman Capote read it, he said, "That isn't writing; it's typing."

Many times in my life, I've had people compare what I did traveling to *On the Road*. Most of the people hadn't read the book— they just knew the reference and what it represented. Bob Dylan, Jerry Garcia, the Beatles, and the Doors all claimed the book greatly influenced them. Many believe the drugs, sex and poetry in the book completely summed up the Beat Generation. The book also featured real people; Dean Moriarty was based on fellow beatnik Neal Cassady.

I'm feeling uneasy about the traffic and wish I'd stopped in New Hampshire. My heart is racing. And having Kerouac bouncing around in my head isn't helping. I slam on the brakes when someone stops short in front of me, and then I hear a voice from my back seat.

The only people that interest me are the mad ones, mad to talk,
desirous of everything at the same time, the ones that never
yawn or say a commonplace thing, but burn, burn, burn
like Roman candles across the night.

I don't have to look in the rearview mirror to know it's Kerouac.

I flip the mirror up so I don't look. I thought I was through with these apparitions, but somehow this fucking guy made it through.

"Shut up!" I shout. Roman gives me a nervous glance, although I probably blend in fine with the frantic drivers around me. I was interested in what Everett Ruess and Edward Abbey had to say, and some of the others as well—but I've got no interest in Kerouac.

My biggest complaint with *On the Road* was the lack of morals in the characters that Kerouac — or his protagonist, Sal Paradise — idolizes. Dean Moriarty is introduced as a new-age mystic seeking the meaning of life, but he comes across as more of a scumbag, hitting on high school girls after abandoning his job and wife.

I wasn't scared, I was just somebody else, some stranger, and my whole life was a haunted life, the life of a ghost…I was halfway across America, at the dividing line between the East of my youth and the West of my future, and maybe that's why it happened right there and then that strange afternoon.

"Shut up!" I yell again. "You don't get to give excuses! You followed a false prophet while he chased his own selfish desires. Call it what you want, but it's not justification for sketchy behavior."

I try to calm down after that. I've got three daughters, and people who prey on young girls trigger me. Not that my girls couldn't handle guys like him. Numbers 1 and 3 would kick his ass, and Number 2 would see him coming a mile away.

I hear no more comments from the back seat — and I don't look.

Why is this happening again? I ask myself. Is it just the traffic? Or the exhaustion from all the driving? I can't go on like this.

I've slowed, and cars are angrily passing me on both sides.

I take a deep breath.

This is because of imbalances in my life. It is my creation. I don't have to exist with these arguments in my head. I wonder if my reading list was the germ of it all.

No, thoughts and ideas by themselves aren't bad.

I drift back to Thoreau and wonder if he had any other words on dealing with your baggage and find the following:

However mean your life is, meet it and live it; do not shun it and call it hard names. It is not so bad as you are. It looks poorest when you are richest. The fault-finder will find faults even in paradise. Love your life, poor as it is. You may perhaps have some pleasant, thrilling, glorious hours, even in a poorhouse.

On I-95 N, I flow due north with the traffic, surrounded by others who want to get away from the cities before the evening commuters. It's a little after 4:00 pm, and I figure once I cross into Maine, I'll find a place along the coast and rest for a bit — maybe get a meal.

There's an eighteen-mile stretch of the highway that passes through New Hampshire, and before I'm done, I go through a toll booth with a massive liquor store behind it. Interesting priorities, New Hampshire.

Still, I'm surprised I feel so nostalgic just by driving through the state I grew up in. I don't think it was the toll booth or the liquor store. And as much as I enjoyed growing up in the Granite State and still have a lot of friends there, I'm not a flag-waving New Hampshirite. It's a beautiful place to live — I could just never settle down there.

But maybe I should be a little more optimistic about the state I grew up in. As I continue, I think of all the good people I knew there over the years, separated now only by my eternal restlessness.

Steinbeck clears his throat and speaks up from the back of my mind, and I let it slide.

I wonder how many people I've looked at all my life and never seen.

I remember a few years back, calling my brother in a fit of depression and asking him if he minded if I came back. He'd laughed whole-heartedly and said, "Nobody said you had to leave in the first place."

My parents' former home overlooking the Nashua River.

Joseph Campbell
(1904 – 1987)

American Literary Nomads

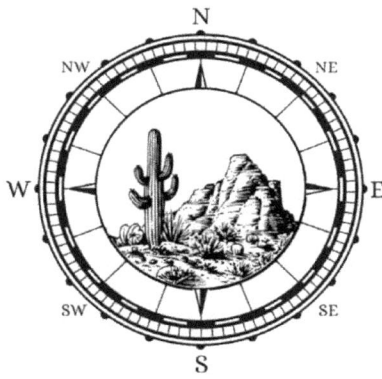

Mount Katahdin, northern Maine.

Chapter Ten

MAINE

I cross the big bridge—the Piscataqua River Bridge—and then I'm in Maine! My final state on what must be about a four-thousand-mile journey. I think back and realize I've just entered my twentieth state on this trip!

I recollect the outing's beginning in Sedona, with Steinbeck bouncing around my head. I feel like I've bonded with him a little, although because he took three months for his journey, and mine will end after a few weeks, I feel like he's still got one up on me. I guess that begs the question: Is this a one-way trip? I'm not sure if I'm ready to go back and face that medicine wheel yet.

Steinbeck claimed his hometown often hated him. I wouldn't go that far; in fact, I've always felt nothing but support from the people of Hollis, New Hampshire. Maybe they didn't quite understand me, but apparently, I don't understand me very well either.

I guess it's best to continue the journey—literary or not. Steinbeck started with *The Grapes of Wrath* in 1939 and ended with *Travels with Charley* in 1962. Neither book represents the America you would see now, but that's not the point. There's an "America" out there waiting to be found—a new one that's being constantly rewritten.

And Steinbeck knew new generations would rediscover it because,

Every American hungers to move.

I've got about four hours to go, but my back is aching, so after about twenty-five miles, I pull into the Kennebunk rest area. Roman is suddenly hopping all over the front seat, and I realize I've neglected him.

I let him pee and run around while I do some squats and pushups. He's on the retractable leash, which he is dragging around in the grass, but it keeps him humble, and he doesn't run off. There are no other dogs here, and we are away from the cars.

He's full of crazy energy, as if the scent of the pines is acting like catnip to him. Despite my aches and pains, I also feel a surge of power. I'm beyond tired, but it's as if I'm in some sort of tractor beam that's just pulling me along. I don't mind letting it—but I've gotta change my pace. At this stage, you must slow down as if time doesn't matter. You have to travel, not commute.

I reduce speed with everything I do as I move toward Roman. I breathe deeper and look around—seemingly for the first time—at the other cars and drivers around the rest area. The sun is behind the pines, toward the horizon. There's a moist, salty odor in the air, and I wonder if I'm close enough to smell the ocean. I hear a raven clucking from an old pine that towers above me…

That change of perspective fills me with joy—the old joy that I thought I'd left behind: the joy of travel and spending time on the road, the joy of watching the sun rise or set with loved ones, the joy of listening to my daughters laughing in the other room, or smelling my wife's neck.

Sorry to ramble, but I haven't seen "joy" in a while.

If I were a happier person, I might whistle.

It amazes me that all I had to do to attain it was slow down.

Maybe I'm finally hitting a pace I might walk that medicine wheel with. But what about intention?

I think of Joseph Campbell and his hero's journey again and wonder what stage I'm in now. Campbell outlined seventeen stages that could also be broken down into three main sections: departure, initiation, and return.

When I entered Maine, you would think I'd be in the fifteenth stage, Crossing the Return Threshold, but something still feels off. That stage refers to returning from the "special" world to the "ordinary" world, bringing back whatever wisdom or boon you gained on your journey. The biggest challenge of this stage is adjusting to the mundane realities of ordinary life after such extraordinary experiences and communicating what you've learned to others.

I'm not ready for any of that. When I think of my journey, all I see are flashes of places. I guess that means I'm still on the journey—and when I close my eyes, I still feel like I'm doing seventy, so that makes sense. Plus, I'm nowhere near ready to talk to anyone else about the craziness that's reigned in my mind over the last few weeks—months.

I am feeling better, but I'm happy to remain mute.

I think of Campbell's list again and decide I must be earlier on his list. I know stage nine is Atonement with the Father, like Luke Skywalker and Darth Vader, but my dad is gone now, and we have no issues. The next stage, stage ten, is called Apotheosis and represents the hero's ultimate transformation and transcendence, where they achieve a higher state of being.

To be honest, that seems a bit lofty to me right now. I forget about the Hero's Journey and instead focus on simply completing a long road trip.

I grab some chicken nuggets at Burger King, which I split with Roman. "Thanks, Bro—you really do love me," he says with his eyes while swallowing them without chewing.

I chide him. "You really should enjoy your food more."

Back in the Buick, I get up to speed and think about Thoreau who was conflicting when he talked about Maine. I may have issues with him, but because of his pure love of the Maine woods, I'll forgive him anything.

He believed the dense forests of northern Maine were wild, largely unexplored, and saturated with the past. He even claimed that they "had never been seen by a white man before." Yet he also pointed out that they were "only a matter of hours from easily accessible Bangor."

I think he was enchanted by the wilderness but also afraid of it, and he wanted his readers to feel that fear.

Some hours of travel north of Bangor will carry the curious to the verge of a primitive forest, more interesting, perhaps, on all accounts, than they would reach by going a thousand miles westward.

That's only Ohio and a bit of a stretch, but he did his best. He was one of the earliest recorded climbers of Mount Katahdin, although he most likely didn't reach the peak, and his 325-mile journey on the Allagash River was ambitious and arduous by any standard.

He published *Walden* in 1854 and *The Maine Woods* ten years later, when he was forty-seven. Despite his enthusiasm, Thoreau seemed lost in the deep woods, and his experience led him to believe he could never live there alone.

Nature was here, something savage and awful, though beautiful... This was that Earth of which we have heard, made out of Chaos and Old Night. Here was no man's garden...

Yet we forgive Thoreau for his exaggerations because, from his observations, he took a leap—and America followed. During his three trips to Maine, he witnessed how loggers, settlers and missionaries were changing the area beyond recognition. He saw the Indian way of life and the vast forest as doomed if we didn't do something.

Thoreau was ahead of his time in condemning river damming and denouncing loggers. He believed land should be set aside and even specified that it should be in national parks.

A pine cut down, a dead pine, is no more a pine than a dead human carcass is a man. Every creature is better alive than dead, men and moose and pine-trees, and he who understands it aright will rather preserve life than destroy it.

And you can feel his frustration with the loggers in lines like:

The wilderness feels... ten thousand vermin gnawing at the base of her noblest trees.

My apologies if I drifted too deeply into Thoreau. These Maine woods line the highway, and I'm tempted to pull over, park, and inhale deeply. Thoreau documented the change in the American forest, especially the northeast, and at the same time showed us how to write about nature. How to care about it, learn about it, and even live alongside it.

Our life should be lived as tenderly and daintily as one would pluck a flower.

His legacy surfaced in me unknowingly when I first read *The Giving Tree*, written and illustrated by Shel Silverstein. The story, which follows the relationship between a young boy and a tree, is an example of a destructive friendship and also of how thoughtlessly we've treated the natural world.

Every day the boy would come to the tree to eat her apples, swing from her branches, or slide down her trunk... and the tree was happy. But as the boy grew older he began to want more from the tree, and the tree gave...

First, the tree gives away its fruit, and then its wood, to please the boy until he is only a stump. Even as a kid, I thought, why not just plant twenty other apple trees and sell all the fruit rather than cutting down the tree?

So, I'm going to put this on the bad book list with *On the Road*.

Don't use your friends until they are spent, regardless of how much you need them or what they offer. It's *On the Road* all over again.

But it's too late on the journey for negativity, so I will focus on the road for a while and try to let the miles tick past.

I approach the second rest area near Cumberland and stop. My wife grew up near here and worked in the Burger King at the rest area when she was young. I like to think our paths crossed a few times on my early runs to the cabin with my parents.

But back then, I always passed by this area with trepidation because of its proximity to Yarmouth, which I was convinced was populated with vampires.

In 1975, Stephen King came out with his second novel, *Salem's Lot*. I read this book when I was twelve, initially in New Hampshire and then on our land in Maine during the first summer when we camped in the open while building the cabin. Even before we went to Maine, it freaked me out. In 1976, while I was reading the book in my parent's basement, a minor earthquake shook our house.

I remember screaming because I thought only my bed was shaking — and it was because of the book — and then feeling intense relief when I discovered the whole house had trembled and my mom had felt it too.

I'll take dealing with an earthquake over facing vampires any day. If I'm being honest, I still feel that way.

In *Salem's Lot*, the protagonist, Ben Mears, returns to his hometown, hoping to cast out his personal demons and shake his past. Unknowingly, he stumbles upon a coven of Vampires.

This was King's second novel after *Carrie*, establishing him as a master of American horror. Unfortunately for me, it made the old Bram Stoker vampires more accessible — and believable — and what better place for them to live than Maine?

When we camped under the stars, my eyes often scanned the edge of the fields where the vampires might hide in the shadows of the trees. In one of the first encounters with the vampire in Salem's Lot, two people suddenly become aware he is near — and this scene alone captures how I felt night after night while my eyes scanned the woods.

They found themselves listening to the silence, fascinated by it. There did not even seem to be the faint, high hum that comes in utter stillness, the sound of nerve endings idling in neutral. There was only a great dead sound-lessness and the beat of blood in their own ears.

And yet they both knew, of course. They were not alone.

Most of King's early work takes place in Maine. The town of Derry, where a few stories overlap, is based on Bangor, Maine. On our way to the cabin, we passed both Bangor and Yarmouth, and when I was a kid, I always slunk down low in my seat when we did.

Our place is one hundred miles north of Bangor; a hundred miles further into the remote, crazy Maine woods. A hundred miles crazier than even Stephen King.

As my dad's Maine friend, Deadeye, always said, "You get in trouble up here, there's nobody comin' to save you."

You were alone — a thought that terrified me when I eyed the dark woods. Again, King understood that fear well.

Alone. Yes, that's the key word, the most awful word in the English tongue. Murder doesn't hold a candle to it, and hell is only a poor synonym.

Before I drive again, I decide to straighten up the front of *the Heat.* It's a mess, and not finding things bothers me when I'm driving; plus, this is part of my "slowing down" process. So, I pull up to a picnic table set under a streetlight, and it only takes a few trips to drag my stuff there so I can pick up the trash on the floor.

197

On the last trip, I carry over my milk crate filled with books. I've been obsessed with these authors and their road trips for the last few years. I thought doing so might get me out of my head—silly, I know now. I've only delved deeper when I passed places that had a connection.

But still, we had our moments.

Now, however, I suddenly feel ready to move on. For better or worse, I think I can get by now without their words of wisdom ringing in my head—or even worse, sounding in my ears like they were with me. That happened for a while and can't be a sign of a healthy mind.

I flip through the books: Ruess and Abbey, Pirsig, Campbell and Whitman, Twain, Hemmingway, and Thoreau… they were solid friends when I needed them. With sage advice, I do have to admit. I clean out the car, toss the trash, and then shuffle everything back except the crate of books.

A young guy is lingering by his car about twenty feet away. He's wearing a *Nirvana* concert t-shirt, although he's too young to ever have seen them. I wonder what he's up to until he pulls a few hits off a vape pen. He seems a little casual about it until I remember it's legal in Maine now. He watches me in silence.

Nirvana! Now, there's a band that saved me. When I returned from traveling in the eighties and early nineties, I discovered the bars in Nashua—like Martha's Exchange—had been taken over by horrible dress codes. I was never a fan of men's fashion back then, and I couldn't believe the same bars I'd been drinking in for years now wanted me to wear sporty little ties and button-up shirts.

Then Grunge burst on the scene after spreading from the Seattle area. Bands like Nirvana, Pearl Jam, Soundgarden, and Alice in Chains created a distinct sound by combining punk metal and indie rock. Even better was the no-frills attitude these guys expressed by performing in t-shirts and torn-up jeans.

Suddenly, my broke-ass collection of clothes was in style.

Even better were the lyrics. The raw honesty and emotional vulnerability in Kurt Cobain's lyrics made him feel like kin to me. He wasn't a traveler, as far as I knew, but he understood the angst and alienation that goes with life on the road. Being an outcast in your own town isn't all that different than being a stranger in another place.

It didn't seem so different from Whitman telling others to celebrate themselves — to take pride in their uniqueness — except maybe some pent-up anger gave the music that hard drive.

I'm so ugly, that's okay, 'cause so are you, we broke our mirrors
Sunday mornin' is every day for all I care and I'm not scared
Light my candles in a daze 'cause I've found God

Those lyrics might not mean much to you, but they rocked my world. I wave goodbye to the kid, take one last look at the milkcrate — and decide to leave it. I do consider grabbing Thoreau's *The Maine Woods* just because I'm finally here, but in the end, I leave it as well. I guess I can ponder it fine without a hard copy.

As I climb into the car, the kid stares at me.

"You leaving those books?" he asks.

I smile. "Yeah, I'm done with them.

He walks over, examines one, takes it, looks at another, and takes that as well. "You sure?" he asks again. "There's some good stuff here."

"All yours," I say, feeling a glow as he picks up the milk crate and carries it to his car. I glance at his t-shirt again and can hear Kurt Cobain singing *Oh Me* accompanied by an acoustic guitar.

If I had to lose a mile. If I had to touch feeling.
I would lose my soul. The way I do.

I don't have to think. I only have to do it.
The results are always perfect. But that's old news.

Back on I-95, my mind goes through a little panic, as if the milk crate is a piece of me I can't live without. I know that's my ego talking, trying to convince me that those objects enhance me and that I need them. It might have worked a month ago, but not today.

I'm in Maine now, and for better or worse, when I get to the cabin, I'll have to deal with my conflicts by myself. Sort that shit out. The sad truth is that it's not worth returning to Arizona if I don't.

The land isn't open here, like out west, and the sunset is barely visible behind the trees. I figure it'd only take an hour to get to the coast and back, but it's too late in the day to make detours.

Still, I imagine standing by the Atlantic — maybe shouting to the Heavens that I made it. I no longer feel the need to scream at God, like I did in Sunset Crater, but maybe instead, I could try Whitman's barbaric yawp!

He described the *"yawp"* as "a primal, unrestrained, and untranslatable vocalization," and that's right up my alley.

Maybe in the coming days, after I've settled into the cabin.

In the back of my mind, I hear Hemmingway whisper, *"You can explore the swamp on another day…"*

We cruise along, Roman and I, as the sky darkens. He's asleep in the passenger seat, not concerned about our destination — not that he even knows we have one. I'm sure he'd be equally excited if we pulled up at the cabin or our home in Sedona and not surprised by either destination.

How do I tap into that willingness to accept whatever comes my way? I remember an Abbey quote, and I'm glad it comes from my memory, not an apparition in the back seat.

All one to me — sandstorm or sunshine, I am content, so long as I have something to eat, good health, the earth to take my stand on, and light behind the eyes to see by.

I do feel much better than when I left Arizona. I'm not always locked in my head, and the chatter has stopped.

I almost miss my writer friends at this point.

This time alone has quieted things for me. For some reason, it has helped me accept some things and let go of others. My past has faded into stories again, not horrible, scars that won't heal. And I guess that goes for the Butcher as well. As crazy as he was, his ghosts can't seem to survive in the east—apparently, he's location-bound.

And Benny and my mom? I can only assume that they are at peace—or I guess I am—because when I think of them now, it's only to reminisce.

Overall, if I'm going to be honest with myself—and at this point, why not?—I like my life. Funny how impossible it would have been for me to say that a few weeks ago.

We pass Augusta, and then Bangor and King's books float by: *Carrie (1974), Salem's Lot (1975), The Shining (1977), The Stand (1978), The Dead Zone (1979), Firestarter (1980),* and *Cujo (1981).* There are many more, of course, but for now, I'm only concerned with the books I read at the cabin. These stories fascinated me and opened new worlds—even if they scared me.

Ironically, as we pass Bangor, I see a guy standing on the street who seriously looks like a vampire with a mullet. The mullet alone was scary, but the guy had a weird stare, too.

Anyway, I will keep moving. I'm less than a hundred miles from the cabin now, and I'm probably better off not thinking about vampires and scary stories before I go off to stay alone in a remote log cabin.

A part of me feels I should have included some modern writers. There are certainly plenty of them. I thought of *Blue Highways* (1982) by William Least Heat-Moon, a soul-searching journey across America using only lesser roads. Or *The Lost Continent* (1989) by Bill Bryson. In this travelog, Bryson tours America, looking for the perfect small town after spending two years in England. These books show the States similarly to Steinbeck's *Travels with Charley*: clearly, with less emotional baggage or stimulants than I put you through.

Another book I didn't mention but thought worthy was *Ghost Rider*, by Neil Peart, the drummer and lyricist for the band Rush.

This philosophical travel memoir follows his 55,000-mile motorcycle journey across North America. It's a powerful read.

I also considered people who dove into the land a bit more deeply, like John Krakauer in *Into the Wild* (1996), which documents Christopher McCandless' ultimately doomed foray across the western United States, or Cheryl Strayed's *Wild*, where she retells her journey along the Pacific Coast Trail in 1995. These books made me want to do more than leave home — they made me want to leave civilization altogether.

But we've only got so many pages here, and I've rambled enough.

Shortly before the Millinocket exit, I glimpse Mount Katahdin looming to the west. I can only see its silhouette, but I well remember standing on the peak and walking the knife's edge.

I feel its power even in the dark, even from this distance.

I'll give you one last quote for our journey, from Thoreau, of course. When he stood before the great mountain, he was instantly confronted by his own mortality.

What a place to live, what a place to die and be buried in!

A month ago, I might have associated that thought with suicide, but on this day, I only want to walk that ridgeline again — maybe this time with a daughter or two.

I miss them with an aching that's seldom quenched. How can you ever survive your babies growing up? Oh, how I wish I could go back in time. But I'm regressing again — what I should wish for is to be with them in the present moment.

To watch Number 1 with her daughter and relish that instant, or spend time on quiet hikes in Sedona with Number 2. And maybe it's time Number 3 and I took another road trip — or maybe we walk that medicine wheel together.

My stomach growls, and I begin to think about food. I have no groceries, and the cabin is only stocked with rice and some canned goods. It's after 8 p.m., and Jerry's in Island Falls will be closed by now, but there's a restaurant up the road that stays open until 9:00 p.m., and I drive there.

I pull into the A Place to Eat and park. My parents came here for twenty years and tried to get a meal here whenever they could. I'm reminiscent as I stare from the parking lot. Roman snores in the driver's seat, and I cover him with a flannel shirt before going inside.

A young waitress with a nametag that reads "Lindsay" seats me and, after a few minutes, takes my order. I still feel like I'm doing 70 mph and can't find my tongue, but I eventually get my order out.

She then returns to the counter to talk to an older woman I recognize from when I came here with my parents. I dig into my memory and remember her name, Brenda, and that she is also the owner.

The two talk casually while the younger one continuously glances at the clock. A truck pulls up, and Lindsay looks at the clock again and sighs. Brenda smiles and tells her to go.

I watch this all, feeling like I'm in Hemingway's *A Clean, Well-Lighted Place*, although the dynamics are slightly different. But it's a good distraction from the road and keeps my mind off the highway while I eat my cheeseburger.

Which is damn good.

Eventually, I request my check.

"You up visiting your camp?" asks Brenda.

I nod. It's just about 9:00 p.m., and everyone else is gone. There's just me, the older waitress and a cook in the back. She turns off the coffee machine on her way back to the register.

Before she returns to my table, she disappears into the back.

When she returns, she holds a big piece of pie in a to-go box.

"Would you mind taking this with you?" she asks. "I baked it myself this morning and just hate to throw it out."

I stare at it—unbelievingly—as the most beautiful slice of apple pie I have ever seen stares back at me. I must be sporting a confused expression because she quickly adds, "There were two slices, but I packed one for my husband as well—and that man does not need two slices of pie before he goes to bed tonight—so you'd be doing me a favor."

I nod again and take out my wallet to add something to my bill, but she kindly stops me, "Oh, heavens no—it's on the house."

I return to the Buick, Roman waking and going crazy for the French fries he smells in my pocket. We take the Island Falls exit and drive for about ten minutes until we reach Winding Hill Road.

The paved portion of the road has four hills in a row. Our cabin is on the top of the third. I cruise along slowly, enjoying the starlit fields that line the road. Halfway there, I glimpse three deer standing beneath a pine tree, watching me pass.

I reach our property and park before a chain that stretches across the driveway. I know where the key is hidden, and I've got my own keys to the cabin, but I just sit here for now.

The cabin is barely visible ahead of me. Built more than fifty years ago by my father and a group of his friends, it has seen some of my life's best and worst times, and I'm hoping I'm ready for it. I take a deep breath.

The apple pie sits next to me, and even though I'm not hungry anymore, I open it to sneak one little bite. And it's delicious. Right up there with my mom's apple pies, which I haven't had in years.

My entire mouth tingles.

Apple-fucking-pie! Who would have thought a piece of pie could taste so good? For some reason, I suddenly, unexpectedly burst into tears. I have three more bites in quick succession.

The sugar—and a little cinnamon—surges through me. It is the last boost I need to drag my tired body from the car. All that's left now is to stumble up the driveway, throw a couple of clean sheets on the bed, and sleep. I'll unlock the gate, move the car up, and unload in the morning.

I grab the camp keys and my phone and notice a text message from my wife. "Call me when you can."

I take a deep breath, knowing this step is as important as the ones leading to the cabin. It's time to face all of my fears. I dial her number, and when she answers the phone, I manage to say, "Hi."

Robert & Roman

Author's note

Illegitimi non carborundum

(Don't let the bastards grind you down.)

*D*espite appearances, this story is about looking for something, not fleeing a thing. There's a great tradition in American literature concerning searching "the open road" for answers and our narrator is just another victim of that Siren's call. The protagonist may stagger out the door unprepared and unsure of his destination, but he is still like Odysseus, hoping to return a better person—if he survives the trials and tribulations.

You may read this story and think it's about a broken heart, but it's not that either. My despair began long before we had issues. I drove myself to be an anxiety-ridden creature by worrying about bills, Climate Change, politics, Covid and everything else.

I let myself be consumed by fear and spent progressively more and more time worrying about the future and less living in the present. I imagine these days it's not so different for many American men—and women—but I also had a solid foundation of past fear and trauma to build on, which amplified things.

I've had my fair share of harrowing experiences traveling and working as a journalist over the years. More than once, I've waited through what I thought were to be my final hours. Twice, I've had someone point a gun at me, empty it, and somehow emerged unharmed.

I've been scared so badly I thought that alone would kill me.

And probably the most detrimental thing are a few of the truly bad humans I've encountered. People who I could only call "evil" — a few of whom I barely escaped. I still see a few of them in crowds — one in particular — although, as you will soon learn, I can't always trust my observations.

Over time, these traumatic experiences have become stories I can recount, and I'm pretty good at telling tales, but the dark roots remain. And telling a thing over and over makes it come alive. I sense these bad characters watching me from the peripherals when I'm weak or tired, and I know it's because I breathed life into them.

Over the coming months, I spent more and more time locked in this delusional state, regretting decisions or fearing what was to come — and occasionally seeing these apparitions. These echoes of my past wouldn't let me be — they just played relentlessly.

Last year, to process it all, I immersed myself in books by American authors who had undertaken their own journeys of exploration on U.S. soil. While the reading provided some solace, it also sank me deeper into my mind, leaving me isolated. Soon, my world revolved around their journeys across America and the series of connected highways they used.

Yet, these authors helped and offered me guidance through words I knew well. I let them ease me along; it seemed a minor thing. Suddenly, I found I could shake off some of the small stuff and deal with the seemingly normal day-to-day — only now I had imaginary friends.

Not wanting my family or friends to see the cracks emerging, I decided to take a road trip and try to process it — and that's when the medicine wheel kicked me out.

This book is Dedicated to two of my favorite people.

Rick "Benny" Fischer
(1964-2023)

and

Patricia Catherine Soper DeMayo
(1943-2023)

Rick "Benny" Fischer
(1964-2023)

Patricia Catherine Soper DeMayo
(1943-2023)

Winding Hill Road, Maine.

Robert Louis DeMayo

Illustrations
(by Tom Fish)

Chapter One – Sedona   John Steinbeck

Chapter Two – Arizona   Everett Ruess

Chapter Three – Utah   Edward Abbey

Chapter Four – Colorado   Robert Pirsig

Chapter Five – North Dakota   Theodore Roosevelt

Chapter Six – Iowa   Walt Whitman

Chapter Seven – Kansas   Mark Twain

Chapter Eight – Ohio   Ernest Hemmingway

Chapter Nine – Massachusetts   Henry David Thoreau

Chapter Ten – Maine   Joseph Campbell

Author's Note   Robert & Roman

Arches National Park.

Acknowledgments

I am indebted to all the friends and strangers who helped me when I was on the road, not just for this book but during my many journeys across America. I might complain about folks at times, but people are the best part of this great land, and be it Alaska, Maine, Arizona or anywhere between those places, I've always been made to feel welcome. This thing with Bill was a one-off.

I'm also grateful for those around me in Sedona who helped me keep my sanity, be it a slow walk around the neighborhood, a treatment by the talented therapists at Uptown Massage, or a class at Hot Yoga. I can't thank you all enough.

I need to mention Hot Yoga again and its owner, Jennifer Richards: Thank you for your positive energy and narration. Thank you for creating such a constructive, healing environment, which helped me get out of my head daily. You and all your instructors have been a big part of my transformation from a stressed-out, out-of-shape guy to someone who looks forward to each day. Thank you, Layna Cirelli, for your years of helping me rebuild me back, and Soña Hernandez, Elena Larsen, Nicole Tierre and Dani Butterly for the journeys I've gone through in your classes, too!

Thank you, Mark Patton, for your advice and tour guide services when I passed through Chanute, Kansas. Thanks, Chris and Margie Fitzpatrick, for putting me up in the she-shed for a night. And thank you, brother Dave, for always having a room for me whenever I crash-landed in New Hampshire. Special thanks to Drew Trabish for driving up to Arches and Canyonlands in Utah when I was researching this book—what a place to visit off-season!

Thank you, Christopher O'Brian, Ph.D., at the Theodore Roosevelt Center in Dickenson, N.D., for helping me understand TR's state of mind when he arrived in the Badlands. Thank you, Medora Riding Stables, for getting me in a saddle and out on the land a few times. One of the highlights of my visit to TR National Park was my time on horseback.

A special thanks to Andy Anderson, who plowed me out and delivered wood when I got snowed in at the Maine cabin while trying to finish this novel. No snow all winter, then three feet in my first two weeks there. Ha! But I caught the eclipse from the porch.

I am so excited to feature Tom Fish's artwork in this novel and want to thank him for his incredible efforts. I would also like to thank Andrew Holman for his photos and for creating the cover.

I want to thank my mother for inspiring me to go to North Dakota, Benny Fischer for the books he recommended and his enthusiasm as we planned that excursion together before his passing, and his wife, Colette Fischer, for her assistance with details about Benny's life while I was writing this book.

Thank you, Ky and Moon McMillan, for the awesome compass logo. Also, thank you, Claire Obermarck, for your honest and insightful comments on earlier drafts. There's nothing better than good criticism. Thank you, Bob Brill, for your comments, edits and helpful advice throughout the writing of this book.

Lastly, I want to thank Diana DeMayo and my three daughters, Tavish, Saydrin and Martika. I mention their names now because they deserve recognition for all their attempts to keep me on track. My daughters also helped create the eBook and are now part of my publishing process. Thank you also for always encouraging me and making me feel like muses surround me.

Robert Louis DeMayo and family. 2019.

The author at America's Stonehenge, Salem, N.H.

Biography

R*obert Louis DeMayo* is a native of Hollis, N.H., but traveled through many corners of the planet before settling in the Southwest. He took up writing at the age of twenty when he left his job as a biomedical engineer to explore the world. Over a ten-year period—the last decade before the internet—DeMayo completed ten six-month trips abroad and visited close to 100 countries, crossing many of them overland.

His extensive journaling during his travels inspired four of his novels and far-reaching work for the travel section of *The Telegraph*, out of Nashua, NH, as well as the *Hollis Times*. He is a longtime member of The Explorers Club and chair of its Southwest Chapter.

His undying hunger for exploration led to a job marketing for Eos Study Tours, a company that served as a travel office for six non-profit organizations and offered dives to the *Titanic* and the *Bismarck*, Antarctic voyages, African safaris and archaeological tours throughout the world.

For several years after that, Robert worked as a tour guide in Alaska, during the summers, leading hikes and horseback excursions in the Yukon, and as a jeep guide in Arizona during the winter. He was made general manager of the Arizona Jeep tour company but eventually left the guiding world to write full-time.

The last few years have seen him exploring US soil, usually for writing projects, in Utah's Zion, Arches and Canyonlands National

Parks, Sedona and the Verde Valley, Hawaii, the Badlands of North Dakota, and Aroostook County in northern Maine.

DeMayo is the author of eight novels: *The Making of Theodore Roosevelt*, a fictionalized account of Roosevelt´s first acquaintance with wilderness living; *The Light Behind Blue Circles*, a mystery thriller set in Africa; *The Wayward Traveler*, a semi-autobiographical story following a young traveler on his adventures abroad; *Pledge to the Wind, The Legend of Everett Ruess*, a fictionalized account of the life and times of the young solo traveler of the American West; *The Road to Sedona*, the story of a young family that heads up to Alaska to find work in the wake of 9/11; *The Sirens of Oak Creek*, a historical mystery of Oak Creek Canyon, Arizona spanning twelve centuries. Plus *Pithecophilia*, a collection of stories of ape encounters, and *The King of the Coral Sea*, a historical fiction account of Michael Fomenko's great sea journey. Collectively, his books have won a dozen national awards.

This November, he will publish *American Literary Nomads* and, the next fall, a historical mystery in Maine entitled *Winding Hill Road*.

Currently, he resides in Sedona, AZ, and spends his time with his three daughters: Tavish Lee, Saydrin Scout, and Martika Louise.

Books by Robert Louis DeMayo

Nonfiction Travelogue

The Wayward Traveler
(978-0983345398)

The Road to Sedona
(978-0991118359)

Pithecophilia
(978-0998439181)

American Literary Nomads
(979-8989343003)

Poetry & Prose

Random Thoughts from the Road
(978-0983345343)

Historical Fiction

The Making of Theodore Roosevelt
(978-0983345312)

The Legend of Everett Ruess
(978-099118311)

The King of the Coral Sea
(978-0998439198)

Historical Mysteries

The Light Behind Blue Circles
(978-0983345350)

The Sirens of Oak Creek
(978-0998439136)

Coming Soon

Aroostook Dreams
(979-8989343010)

Also by Robert Louis DeMayo

THE LEGEND OF EVERETT RUESS

In this compelling narrative, Robert Louis DeMayo has taken journal excerpts, poems, and letters Everett sent to family and friends in the early thirties and turned them into historical fiction. Through this recreation of Everett's travels, we are given rare glimpses of the young artist as he traveled the southwest — much of which was still an unexplored wilderness back then.

Everett traveled alone, accompanied only by a dog named Curly, but he often stayed with Navajo or Hopi. Using only burros or horses, Everett explored much of Utah and Arizona, covering about twenty miles a day. He crossed the Grand Canyon regularly. The Navajo and Hopi that came across him miles from any road thought he was a mystic and called him Picture Man. They allowed him to witness — and participate in — ceremonies that today are mostly off-limits to non-Indians.

Upon reading it, Brian Ruess wrote, "In this work of fiction ... I saw Everett for the first time, as he might actually have been."

Historical Fiction.
Wayward Publishing.
Available in print, eBook
& audiobook.

"This novel affirms the saying that 'all who wander are not lost.' The portrayal of Everett Ruess gives us a beautiful poetic adventure. We feel his urge to be at one with nature and how this becomes his true spiritual home – and possible resting place. It is a gripping tale that any traveler or explorer will relate to and enjoy."
Sally Douglas

Please enjoy this short excerpt from *The Legend of Everett Ruess*

Random Chapter

The Hole-in-the-Rock Trail, Utah
(October 1934)

*E*verett led Cockleburs and Chocolatero over a rocky mesa of sage and snakeweed. They were on an open plain cut by deep ravines, following the Hole-in-the-Wall Trail as it ran south by southeast out of Escalante.

A cold breeze greeted him, and he had his head down.

The Mormon trailblazers who had created this trail had eventually stopped at the town of Bluff, one hundred and eighty miles from Escalante. Everett's destination as he entered this remote wilderness was the Colorado River, about sixty miles away. To his right lay the Kaiparowits Plateau, whose steep canyons drained into the Escalante, and directly south was Glen Canyon.

Late in the afternoon he came upon a gentle stream that flowed by the base of a sandstone cliff, and he prepared camp. "This place looks like it was made for us," he told the burros as he unloaded the saddle and kyacks.

Above them, a towering wall of rock lit up orange and yellow in the afternoon sun. Tall pines grew by the stream and sprouted on the cliff face wherever a small shelf had collected soil. Far up on the top of the wall, he could see stunted, twisted pines that were now highlighted in gold as the sun set.

He made a small fire, boiled water for rice, and tethered the burros with enough lead to move but not get into trouble. He hadn't seen another human since setting foot on the trail, only squirrels, lizards and birds, and he relaxed by the fire, enjoying his solitude.

Later, the fire had died down to glowing embers, and he decided to write in his journal. He sat with it on his lap, watching the night, listening to it breathe around him.

He was about to jot down an entry when he heard Navajo chanting.

It was far off, barely discernable over the chirping of the crickets that lived along the stream. He thought of the young Navajos he had encountered a few nights before.

He leaned forward, opening his ears more. Cockleburs shifted by his side and he shushed him.

Then it came again. There was only one singer. The song seemed muffled and he couldn't make it out, but the hair on the back of his neck stood up. He felt sure it was one used against witches...

Also by Robert Louis DeMayo

THE WAYWARD TRAVELER

A young man searches the pre-internet world for meaning while traveling on an extreme budget in this real-life, coming-of-age story.

The Wayward Traveler follows the adventures of Louis, an American who, in 1985, is determined to travel the world. The story takes place in forty countries and spans ten years: from the deck of a felucca on the Nile to the scorched dunes of India's Thar Desert to the powerful Beni River in the Amazon Basin.

Louis is broke most of the time and spends considerable effort trying to get by. Along the way, he meets other travelers, learns how to get by on the road, and eventually develops a list of Rules for Survival that help him get by. The Rules might seem trivial to someone reading in the safety of their home, but to Louis, they are his compass. *Embrace the Unknown... Choose Your Battles... Don't Chase the Fire...* each one has a story behind it—or, in this case, a Chapter.

These travels occurred before the internet and cell phones shrunk the world to pocket format. Guidebooks were still non-existent for many of the places, and there were still a few dark spots left on the world's maps. Whether you're a traveler or an armchair traveler, this book will make you feel the road.

Non-fiction Travelogue
Wayward Publishing.
Available in print or eBook.

Please enjoy this short excerpt from *The Wayward Traveler*:

Random Chapter

Jaipur, India
(1990)

(After the sandstorm hit in the night - cont…)

Ali came around and filled each of our water bottles from the large plastic jug. We all stared as he poured the last few drops into the canteen he shared with Rawal.

He stated flatly, "There is no more until we cross the old sea."

We mounted the camels and began to travel single-file, heading dead east with the sun rising directly ahead of us. It seemed impossibly large as it quickly leaped into the sky, and the ever-present glare of the sun hurt my eyes so much that I would almost have traded almost anything to have my sunglasses back—but they were lost to the desert with everything else.

I liked Ali and trusted him, but I had to question why we hadn't started earlier. I took the piece of my turban that I'd used for shelter wrapped my burned legs in it, and then unraveled a bit more to shade my eyes.

My mouth had an awful taste in it, and I yearned to brush my teeth, but the sudden sandstorm had taken everything.

My tongue felt thick as it ran across my chapped lips, and I wanted to down the few mouthfuls remaining in my water bottle, but I tried to conserve the water and not drink.

I'd steal a quick sip and swish it in my mouth as long as I could. As Kalu plodded along, I daydreamed about cool, clean water. The thought of a shower was intoxicating. Jita had spoken of the Ganges River, far to the East, and I imagined myself floating in it, letting the healing properties of the water wash over me.

We skirted the base of the dunes and, after about five kilometers, reached the edge of a hard, baked plain. There wasn't

227

a single piece of vegetation in sight. The dunes and the thorny bushes had seemed extremely bleak, but what lay before us was truly daunting. The hard earth below was perfectly—almost unnaturally—flat. I leaned over Kalu's side and saw the ground looked cracked and aged; the camels didn't leave a print on it.

In every direction, the horizon shimmered. I couldn't see across the plain.

"The ancient sea," said Ali.

The deadly vista took my breath away. Even Jita, who'd been radiating a new, sturdy confidence since the sandstorm, seemed intimidated.

"We are to cross this?"

Ali nodded and pointed into the distance. "It is only fifteen kilometers more to the abandoned city—and there is shelter."

"How long will it take to cross?" I asked.

Ali scratched his head. "Thirty minutes."

I stared at the shimmering plain and thought: thirty minutes of exposure compared to two days in this heat. It seemed obvious that we should take the shortcut, but I would guess the temperature would be close to 120 degrees or hotter.

I looked over at the two Austrians. Anton sat slumped in his saddle, pale and sickly. Axel caught me watching and said, "We must get him to shelter. Let's go."

I nodded. "We can do this."

Ali led us into the white hell with the camels moving at a fast trot that jostled us around crazily. The movement hurt my ribs, yet I knew we had no other choice. At this speed, I tried to console myself, we will cross quickly—if we could manage to hold on that long. I tried to make out the abandoned city in the distance before us, but the glare flashed in my eyes, and I had to clamp them shut.

Ten miles to shelter, I thought. I can hold on for ten miles.

Within a few minutes, I lost sight of the scrub brush we'd paused at. Ali got the camels to pick up their pace, and soon we were making our desperate dash. I felt like I was flying…

Milton Keynes UK
Ingram Content Group UK Ltd.
UKHW021924151124
451262UK00014B/1595

9 798989 343041